T0015213

If These **WALLS** *Could* **TALK:**
LOS ANGELES DODGERS

Stories from the Los Angeles Dodgers Dugout, Locker Room, and Press Box

Houston Mitchell

TRIUMPH
BOOKS

Library of Congress has cataloged the previous edition as follows:

Mitchell, Houston.
  If these walls could talk, Los Angeles Dodgers : stories from the Los Angeles Dodgers dugout, locker room, and press box / Houston Mitchell.
    pages cm
  Summary: "Favorite stories and moments in the history of the Los Angeles Dodgers"— Provided by publisher.
  Includes bibliographical references.
  ISBN 978-1-60078-928-1 (pbk.)
  1. Los Angeles Dodgers (Baseball team)—History. 2. Los Angeles Dodgers (Baseball team)—Anecdotes. I. Title.
  GV875.L6M58 2014
  796.357'640979494--dc23

                                                                2013050874

This book is available in quantity at special discounts for your group or organization. For further information, contact:

    Triumph Books LLC
    814 North Franklin Street
    Chicago, Illinois 60610
    (312) 337–0747
    www.triumphbooks.com

Printed in U.S.A.
ISBN: 978-1-63727-305-0
Design by Amy Carter

For Diana, Sabrina, Samantha, Hannah, and Riley,
who fill my heart with joy and made this book possible

CONTENTS

FOREWORD

Yes, this is a book about the Los Angeles Dodgers. But what gives it a unique perspective is that it's not just for Dodgers fans but for anyone who loves baseball.

Houston Mitchell accomplished a difficult task in *If These Walls Could Talk: Los Angeles Dodgers.* He tells us the inside story from the clubhouse and manager's office while also reviewing game and seasonal highlights from many Dodger Blue campaigns.

I appreciate Mitchell's thorough research, which has been done to substantiate the facts of the club's 56 seasons in the City of the Angels. This book is exciting because it is true.

Houston's writing style—short sentences, short paragraphs—makes for a fast read. Never are you bogged down by unnecessary words.

When you finish this book, I think you will agree with me that Houston Mitchell's account helps round out the history of one of the most popular, honored, and valued franchises in sports—the Los Angeles Dodgers.

We've all wondered what we would hear if walls could talk. This book lets us hear them speak.

—*Ross Porter*
Los Angeles Dodgers Play-by-Play Announcer, 1977–2004

PROLOGUE

It was the best of times; it was the worst of times.... No, that's not quite right.

Call me Ishmael.... No, that's not it either.

It was a bright cold day in April, and the clocks were striking thirteen... No, I know I will get this opening right eventually.

He was an old man who fished alone in a skiff in the Gulf Stream and he had gone eighty-four days now without taking a fish... Wow, that's not even close.

Wait, now I know how to start this.

It has been exhilarating and exasperating to be a Dodger fan in the years since the first edition of this book came out in 2014. The Dodgers have easily been the best team in the National League in that time span, but they have only one World Series title.

They have won the NL West eight of nine seasons in that span (and won 106 games the other season), but they have only one World Series title.

They have had multiple MVP Award winners in that span, but—and stop me if you've heard this before—they have only one World Series title.

And that World Series title game after a 60-game, pandemic-shortened season in which 16 teams made the postseason, causing fans of some teams (hello, Giants fans) to say it's not a real title. Even though you know the fine, fine people (is there a sarcasm font?) who support the Giants would claim it as real if they had won.

Also in the ensuing years since the first edition, I have started writing a Dodgers newsletter for the *Los Angeles Times*, who mysteriously continue to employ me. (Self-promotion alert: You can sign up for the newsletter at latimes.com/newsletters/dodgers-dugout—it's free!) So if you bought this book and are a newsletter subscriber: Thanks! If you bought this book and aren't a newsletter subscriber: Thanks! And if you looked at this book in the store and put it down, never to buy it: Thanks (for nothing).

A lot has happened to the Dodgers since the end of the 2013 season. A new manager. The rise and fall of Yasiel Puig. Three World Series appearances. One World Series victory (have I mentioned they've won only one?) A World Series that was stolen from them. The rise and fall of Cody Bellinger. The influx of new arms such as Dustin May, Walker Buehler, and Tony Gonsolin. Kenley Jansen becoming the best closer in team history. That barely scratches the surface.

But perhaps the most important thing to happen to the Dodgers since 2013 didn't even take place on the field: The retirement and death of Vin Scully. There was truly an outpouring of emotion when he died. Thousands of people became Dodgers fans because of him. Thousands of fans grew up falling asleep listening to him. But we'll talk more about that later in this book.

In this edition we will try to catch you up on as much of all of the above as possible, in a section we have cleverly titled "Epilogue."

If you bought this book when it first came out, feel free to skip ahead and join us over there. If you are buying this for the first time, I hope you enjoy the journey toward the Epilogue as much as I have enjoyed writing it. And if you have any questions, comments, or complaints, feel free to email me at Houston.mitchell@latimes.com.

—Houston Mitchell
October 2022

INTRODUCTION

When I was a little kid, I would sit on the front porch of my house while waiting for the school bus to pick me up. Spread in front of me was the sports section of the *Los Angeles Times*. I remember reading that Bill Buckner had been traded and being crushed that one of my favorite Dodgers had been sent away. There was no way I could go to school that day. Mom made me go anyway.

I was fortunate to know what I wanted to do when I was young. I wanted to work for the *Los Angeles Times* sports section, and I wanted to be a writer. I was hired by the *Times* in 1991 and promoted to assistant sports editor in 2009, completing one goal.

The other goal was completed with the book you hold in your hands.

My hope for this book is to remind Dodgers fans of some of the great moments in team history, and hopefully remind you of some forgotten moments. I wanted the stories to be told through the words of the players who took part, bringing back memories of those ancient days when the Dodgers seemed to be in the playoffs every year and they ruled the city. Don't worry, those days will come again.

I tried to approach writing this book through the eyes of a Dodgers fan. If I were picking up a book like this at a store, what stories would I want to see? Which players would I want to hear from? Hopefully, the choices were wise ones.

The L.A. Dodgers have a rich, vibrant history, and it is impossible to include every story in this book, unless you want it to weigh 50 pounds. I apologize if your favorite didn't make the cut this time, but maybe, if there's a sequel, I can include it then.

So, enough with the introduction. You're here to read about the Dodgers. Turn the page. I hope you enjoy.

CHAPTER 1
THE 1950s

Welcome to Los Angeles...

The Brooklyn Dodgers were revered in the New York area, but they were beloved by fewer and fewer people as the years rolled by. In 1957, the team was overshadowed by constant talk of the team's possible move to the West Coast, and owner Walter O'Malley was demanding a new stadium if the team was to remain in Brooklyn.

O'Malley began negotiating for a new stadium in 1953, and his plans included a dome that could be closed if it rained and a seating capacity of 60,000. New York dragged its feet during negotiations, never really believing the Dodgers would leave for the West Coast.

On October 8, 1957, O'Malley announced that after 68 seasons in Brooklyn, the Dodgers would be moving to Los Angeles. Earlier that month, the Los Angeles County Board of Supervisors voted to spend $2.7 million from a gasoline tax fund to build access roads and prepare a section of Los Angeles known as Chavez Ravine for a new stadium that would be built for the Dodgers. When the decision to move to L.A. was announced, the city powers were thrilled.

It's easy to assume now that the move was greeted with great confidence that the Dodgers would be an immediate sensation in L.A. But that was not the case at all, as evidenced by this quote from 1957:

"We are delighted they are going to come," said John Anson Ford, president of the Board of Supervisors. "We hope they'll prove popular. We are relying on Mr. O'Malley's fine reputation to fill the gaps of uncertainty that have been created, and we believe that in the end the community will be deeply gratified."

On April 18, 1958, the Dodgers played their first game in Los Angeles, defeating the Giants 6–5 before 78,672 fans at the Coliseum. Stars on hand included Gregory Peck, Alfred Hitchcock, Burt Lancaster, Jack Lemmon, Nat "King" Cole, future Angels owner Gene Autry, Groucho Marx, Danny Thomas, and John Ford.

Although everything was all smiles that day at the Coliseum, dark clouds were rising not too far away.

...Now Go Home

Construction on Dodger Stadium began in 1958, but there was one problem—a large group of families lived on the site of the future stadium. The city wanted them out.

Lou Santillan was a teenager when his parents were forced out of their home in Chavez Ravine, the hillside area overlooking downtown Los Angeles that would eventually become the home of Dodger Stadium. In all, more than 1,000 mostly Mexican American families from Chavez Ravine were removed from their homes to make way for the stadium. It is still a dark note in Los Angeles history, one many people would like to forget. But not everyone can forget.

This general view shows the crowd of 78,672 at the Los Angeles Memorial Coliseum before game time on Opening Day for the Los Angeles Dodgers on Friday, April 18, 1958. The Dodgers defeated the San Francisco Giants 6–5. *(AP Photo)*

"There's people who won't even step into Dodger Stadium. They're still bitter. My uncle, who was a priest, he wouldn't have gone to any Dodger games," Eddie Santillan told the *Los Angeles Times* in 2012. "But I had no anger or frustration against them. I love the Dodgers. Growing up in L.A., that's our team, you know."

On May 9, 1959, with the team in the middle of a season that would send it to the World Series, the city of Los Angeles evicted all the people living in Chavez Ravine. TV cameras showed it all. Some went peacefully, some had to be dragged away.

It was an ugly start to what turned out to be a great love affair between the city and its team.

The Coliseum

The L.A. Memorial Coliseum is easily the most unusual stadium to play host to Major League Baseball. When the Dodgers moved to Los Angeles, they were without a home. Dodger Stadium wouldn't be ready until 1962. So the L.A. Coliseum, a stadium built for football and home of the 1932 Summer Olympics, was the Dodgers' home for four seasons.

How unusual was the stadium? The home run distance to left was 250', but there was a 40' fence installed to keep players from hitting easy pop-fly home runs. To right field, the fence was 440'. In 1958, only nine home runs were hit in 77 games at the Coliseum.

"It was weird, weird, weird playing in the Coliseum," Dodgers infielder Randy Jackson said in an interview with Don Zminda in 2011.

But there is one player in particular who loved the Coliseum: Wally Moon.

Moon, a lefty, found a way to change his swing and put just the right spin on the ball to lift it high in the air and over the left-field screen. Moon hit 37 home runs in the Coliseum during his Dodgers career, compared to only 12 on the road. Fans took to Moon's slugging prowess so well that they dubbed his homers "Moon Shots."

But perhaps Don Drysdale said it best, "It's nothing but a sideshow. Who feels like playing baseball in this place?"

Roy Campanella Night

Sorry Mike Piazza, but Roy Campanella is the greatest catcher in Dodgers history. A three-time MVP, Campanella was expected to be one of the cornerstones of the team in their first few seasons in Los Angeles. That all changed on January 28, 1958.

Campanella owned a liquor store (these were the days when athletes needed off-season jobs just to make ends meet) in Harlem. On January 28, he closed his store and drove home on a cold winter's evening. While traveling on an S-curve on Dosoris Lane in Glen Cove, New York, his car hit a patch of ice and skidded off the road, overturning and hitting a telephone pole. Campanella suffered a broken neck in the accident, leaving him paralyzed from the shoulders down. While he eventually regained the use of his arms, he was confined to a wheelchair for the rest of his life.

On May 7, 1959, the Dodgers paid tribute to Campanella by holding a special night in his honor before an exhibition game against their old rivals, the New York Yankees. And the people of Los Angeles showed how much they loved their new team and respected the team's legends, as a record 93,103 people showed up for the game and to honor Campanella.

As thousands of lighters illuminated the Coliseum, Campanella was wheeled to home plate by Pee Wee Reese. The microphone was lowered, and the audience remained totally silent as Campanella spoke:

"I thank each and every one of you from the bottom of my heart. This is something I'll never forget as long as I live. I want to thank the

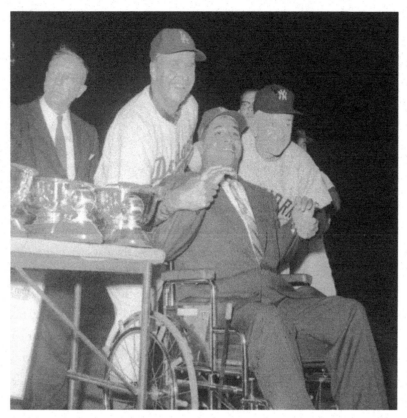

Roy Campanella, the former Dodgers catcher paralyzed in an auto crash, is flanked by Los Angeles Dodgers manager Walt Alston (left) and New York Yankees manager Casey Stengel as he was introduced to the crowd before the start of an exhibition game honoring him in the Los Angeles Coliseum on May 7, 1959. The crowd of 93,103 spectators was the largest in the history of baseball. *(AP Photo)*

Yankees for playing this game, and my old Dodgers team, too. It's a wonderful tribute. I thank God I'm able to be here and see it."

And with that, 93,103 people gave Roy Campanella a standing ovation that lasted for seven minutes. "My legs aren't working, my heart is soaring," Campanella said of the ovation.

Thirty years later, Campanella remembered the game and team owner Walter O'Malley, who was responsible for organizing the special night.

"A lot of people didn't know O'Malley for what he was," Campanella said. "He stood by me every minute after my accident, helping me to see my way through. No one knows that after that wonderful night he had for me in the Coliseum when 93,000 showed up, he gave me a check for $50,000. And he continued my salary, which was more than $50,000 a year, for years after that. He was a great pioneer in integrating baseball."

Don't Pinch Him

Chuck Essegian has one claim to fame—he is one of only two people to hit two pinch-hit home runs in one World Series.

The 1959 World Series matched the Dodgers, in just their second year in Los Angeles, against the Chicago White Sox. The White Sox routed the Dodgers 11–0 in Game 1 and were leading 2–1 with two out in the seventh inning of Game 2 when Essegian turned around the Series.

Dodgers manager Walter Alston sent Essegian to the plate to bat for starting pitcher Johnny Podres. White Sox starter Bob Shaw ran the count to 3–1 when Essegian launched a curve ball halfway up the left-center stands at Comiskey Park, tying the score. Charley Neal homered two batters later, giving the Dodgers a 4–2 lead in a game they won 4–3 to even the Series.

The second home run wasn't quite as dramatic. The Dodgers were leading 8–3 in the ninth inning of Game 6 when Essegian, batting for Duke Snider, homered to left field against Ray Moore.

But to Essegian, those two homers may have ruined his baseball career.

"You know, you kind of get labeled as a certain kind of player," Essegian said when interviewed not long after his career ended in 1963. "If you have success as a pinch-hitter, then you're looked at as a pinch-hitter because you're not good enough to play every day. It's a hard tag to live down."

In 404 major league games, Essegian batted .255 with 47 home runs and 150 runs batted in. His best season was with Cleveland in 1962, when he had 21 homers and 50 RBIs. "For one reason or another, I just never played much in baseball," Essegian said. "It just didn't work out the way I'd hoped it would."

Essegian is one of the few people to play in a Rose Bowl game and a World Series game. He was a linebacker on Stanford's 1952 Rose Bowl team.

In case you were wondering, the other player to hit two pinch-hit home runs in one World Series is Bernie Carbo for the 1975 Boston Red Sox.

CHAPTER 2
THE 1960s

Welcome to Dodger Stadium

The Taj Mahal of Major League Baseball opened for business on April 10, 1962, and players were immediately impressed by the new Stadium.

"It's the most gorgeous thing I've ever seen in my life," shortstop Maury Wills said on opening day. "They've done a wonderful job on it."

Others were just as impressed.

Don Drysdale: "This ball park knocks your eyes out. Beautiful."

Duke Snider: "Being a native of California [Snider was born in Los Angeles], this is really wonderful."

Johnny Podres: "I'll tell you one thing, I'll win some games here."

Commissioner Ford Frick: "Baseball has never had anything like this. It marks the beginning of a new era in baseball."

Reds pitcher Bob Purkey: "There's only one problem. It's ruined one of my best banquet jokes. I used to tell fans that it really wasn't so bad in the Coliseum, that it came in handy along about the seventh inning to be able to rest by reaching out your right hand and leaning back against the left-field screen."

The fans immediately fell in love with the stadium, except for one problem—there were no drinking fountains. One fan in attendance, Rose Hernandez, said she asked a Dodgers employee where she could get a drink of water and was told she could use any of the taps in the ladies' restrooms.

The drinking fountains problem became public when then–City Councilman Edward Roybal pointed out that the L.A. Coliseum, where the Dodgers played from 1958–61, had 150 water fountains and the L.A. Sports Arena, home of the NBA's Los Angeles Lakers and much smaller than Dodger Stadium, had 48. Roybal suggested that perhaps team owner Walter O'Malley was hoping the lack of fountains would drive more people to the concession stands for an ice-cold beer or soda.

O'Malley denied the charge, saying it was just an oversight.

Jim Gilliam slaps a ground ball as the Dodgers and the Cincinnati Reds meet in the first game played at the new 56,000-seat Dodger Stadium in Chavez Ravine near Los Angeles, California, on April 10, 1962. A crowd of 52,564 was on hand as the Reds won 6–3. *(AP Photo)*

For the second home game, on April 11, O'Malley came up with a solution. There were 221 perfectly usable cold-water faucets in the restrooms of the stadium, and the team had purchased Dixie cups to set out in the restrooms.

That didn't really please a lot of people, since drinking water from a bathroom faucet isn't really high on anyone's list of thirst-quenching refreshments. The City Health Department stepped in and ordered O'Malley to install drinking fountains in spectator areas.

And *voila*! Just like that, by the time the next homestand opened in late April, there were 54 drinking fountains.

Dodger Stadium Firsts

The Dodgers played the Reds for the Stadium opener, which the Reds won 6–3 thanks to a three-run homer by Wally Post.

Here are some Stadium firsts:

First hit and first extra-base hit: Cincinnati's Eddie Kasko led off the game with a double.

First run scored: Kasko, who scored in the first on Vada Pinson's single.

First double play: Cincinnati's Frank Robinson, who grounded into a 6-4-3 double play to end the first inning.

First strikeout: Cincinnati's Gordy Coleman was struck out by Johnny Podres in the second inning.

First walk: Cincinnati's Tommy Harper was walked by Johnny Podres in the second inning.

First Dodgers hit: Duke Snider, a single to center in the second.

First homer: Post, his three-run homer in the seventh off Podres.

First Dodgers homer: Jim Gilliam, on April 11, off of Cincinnati's Moe Drabowsky.

Stop, Thief!

Let's get one thing straight right away: Maury Wills should be in the Hall of Fame. He won an MVP Award, but he also made the stolen base a weapon again, and that alone should put him in Cooperstown.

Wills came up to the Dodgers in 1959 and stole seven bases in 83 games. Big deal. In 1960 he led the league with 50 and led again in 1961 with 35. Good, but not earth-shattering numbers, and they are well below the record of 96 set by Ty Cobb in 1915.

And then, in 1962, Wills stole the spotlight.

He stole five bases in the first two games of the season, giving the league fair notice that he was planning to run with abandon. He stole eight bases in April, 19 in May, 15 in June, nine in July, and 22 in August. But in September he really turned it on.

Maury Wills went head first into second base as he stole his 96ᵗʰ base of the season in the third inning of a game against the St. Louis Cardinals at Busch Stadium in St. Louis, Missouri, on September 23, 1962. Cardinals shortstop Dal Maxvill took the late throw. The umpire was Tony Venzon. *(AP Photo)*

In a game against the Cubs in Chicago, he stole second, but the Cubs protested to umpire Jocko Conlan, saying he made the call before the ball even reached the bag.

Conlan replied, "You ain't got him all year. Why would you think you'd get him this time?"

Wills had 95 stolen bases, one away from tying the record, as the Dodgers began a game against the Cardinals on September 23 in St. Louis. Curt Simmons was scheduled to start for the Cardinals.

"The writers were always asking me who was the easiest pitcher to steal off," Wills said in a 2012 interview. "I never told them, but the truth was it was Curt Simmons. I think I could steal off him today."

When the game started, Curt Simmons wasn't on the mound. Larry Jackson was.

"The toughest guy to steal off was Larry Jackson," Wills said. "Suddenly, he was on the mound. I found out later that Simmons had given him the ball. The Cardinals didn't want to give up the record." Wills singled and stole second in the third inning to give him 96 steals, tying Cobb.

"Tying it is nothing," Wills said. "When you get that far, you want it alone."

Wills stayed off the bases until the seventh inning, when he singled with two out and no one on. The whole stadium knew he would go for the record. Larry Jackson knew it, too.

"Jackson threw over to first 16 times," Wills said. "Bill White was the first baseman, and every time I went diving back into first base, he'd slap the ball down hard on my head or face. They were killing me."

It was then that something Dodgers general manager Al Campanis had said to Wills came into his mind.

"It had been just a couple of weeks earlier," Wills said. "Al stopped me on the way in, took me in his office, and reminded me that once in a while I ought to try a delayed steal. We practiced it right there in his office. You take a shorter lead, you make the pitcher think you have given up, that he's won. You don't even break until you see the white of the ball leave the catcher's hand. At that point, the catcher's eyes and infielders' eyes are off you and on the ball. Then you break."

Wills broke and stole second. The record was his. He finished the season playing every inning of the Dodgers' 165 games and stealing 104 bases.

In 1961, the entire National League stole 468 bases. That number rose to 788 in 1962, and in 1970, the NL had 1,045 stolen bases mainly because of Maury Wills, who blazed a new trail for baseball.

Wills spent 15 years on the Baseball Hall of Fame ballot. The highest voting percentage he received was 40.6 percent in 1981 (you need 75 percent to be elected). He dropped off the ballot after the 1992 election, and today his fate rests in the hands of the Classic Baseball Era Committee.

Hopefully, one day it will do the right thing.

Almost, but Not Quite

The 1962 season is one that the Dodgers let get away from them. With seven games remaining, the Dodgers were leading the National League by four games. Then everything fell apart. They lost six of their last seven and were tied by the San Francisco Giants on the final day of the season, necessitating a three-game playoff to determine the NL champion.

But this couldn't end up like 1951, could it? Splitting the first two and leading in Game 3 until the Giants rally to win the pennant? That couldn't happen again, surely. What are the odds?

Game 1 was a laugher for the Giants. Sandy Koufax, who wasn't quite the legendary Sandy Koufax yet, was pelted for three runs in only one inning pitched, came out of the game in the second, and watched from the bench as the Giants ran away with an 8–0 victory at Candlestick Park.

"I had an idea what I wanted to do out there, but I couldn't seem to do it," Koufax said after the game. "I try to throw hard, but the ball doesn't come out hard and my control was way off."

Manager Walter Alston seemed confident. "My theory is that if just one or two guys break loose, we'll catch on fire," Alston told a gathering of reporters after Game 1. "If there's any pressure now, it's on the Giants. We have everything to win and nothing to lose."

The Dodgers' day in San Francisco was summed up perfectly after the game. The police motorcycle escort leading them to the airport got lost and led the Dodger bus into a dead-end street.

That was okay, however, because the last two games would be played at Dodger Stadium with L.A.'s two best pitchers, Don Drysdale and Johnny Podres, on the mound.

Drysdale started Game 2, and it looked like the Giants would run away with it again. Orlando Cepeda singled with one out in the second inning and scored on a double by Felipe Alou. Drysdale settled down until the sixth inning when the Giants made it 2–0 when Tom Haller walked and took third base on a double by Jose Pagan. Giants starting pitcher Jack Sanford bunted, but Drysdale threw the ball away, allowing Haller to score and Pagan to move to third. Chuck Hiller and Jim Davenport followed with singles, and suddenly it was 4–0 with two men on and one out. Ed Roebuck relieved Drysdale and retired the Giants' best hitter, future Hall of Famer Willie Mays, before giving up a single to Willie McCovey to make it 5–0 Giants.

Finally, just as Dodgers fans were thinking of heading for the exits, the Dodgers came alive. Sanford walked Jim Gilliam to open the bottom of the sixth and was relieved by Stu Miller. Big mistake. Miller didn't have a thing. Duke Snider doubled, advancing Gilliam to third. Tommy Davis then hit a sacrifice fly, scoring Gilliam and advancing Snider. Wally Moon walked and Frank Howard singled, scoring Snider to make it 5–2. Billy O'Dell relieved Miller and gave up a single to Doug Camilli, loading the bases. O'Dell then hit Andy Carey with a pitch to force in a run, and it was 5–3. Lee Walls, batting for Roebuck, doubled to clear the bases and give the Dodgers a 6–5 lead.

Former World Series perfect-game pitcher Don Larsen relieved O'Dell and gave up a ground ball to Maury Wills that scored Walls, who had advanced to third on the throw home following his double. The Dodgers did no further damage, but it was suddenly a new series with the Dodgers leading 7–5 heading into the seventh inning.

Alvin Dark was asked why he pulled Sanford from the game so quickly after he had been pitching so well and the Giants manager said, "He had a cold and was pooped."

The Giants cut the lead to 7–6 in the eighth inning, and the Giants loaded the bases with one out when John Orsino hit a sacrifice fly to tie the game at 7–7. And that's the way it stayed until the bottom of the ninth.

Wills and Gilliam walked to lead off the bottom of the ninth, and Dark brought in Gaylord Perry to pitch. Perry would go on to pitch for 22 seasons, win 314 games, and make the Hall of Fame, but he was a mere rookie in 1962.

Darryl Spencer laid down a sacrifice bunt, advancing the runners to second and third. Perry had ample time to throw to third to force out Wills, but he didn't even look that way as he threw to first.

"I thought Perry had a play on me," Wills said after the game. "I was hoping he'd go to first instead."

Mike McCormick, who would go on to win the Cy Young Award in 1967, relieved Perry and intentionally walked Tommy Davis.

Up to the plate stepped Ron Fairly with the bases loaded and one out in the bottom of the ninth. Fairly lofted a fly ball to Mays in center, but Wills barely beat the throw home. The Dodgers won 8–7, and the series was tied 1–1.

"If I had been on third base instead of Wills, we'd still be playing," Fairly said.

Game 2 lasted 4 hours and 18 minutes, breaking the previous record of 4 hours and 2 minutes for the longest nine-inning game in major league history.

Game 3 featured Juan Marichal of the Giants against Johnny Podres. Let's cut right to the chase. The Dodgers led 4–2 going into the top of the ninth inning—a little eerie because the Dodgers had led 4–1 going into the bottom of the ninth in 1951. But Bobby Thomson had long-since retired, so there was nothing to worry about, right?

Ed Roebuck was pitching for the Dodgers, not Ralph Branca, but the result was similar. Matty Alou led off with a single and was forced at second on Harvey Kuenn's grounder. Willie McCovey and Felipe

Alou walked to load the bases. Willie Mays singled off Roebuck's hand, scoring Kuenn. That led to the controversial moment of the inning.

Alston had Stan Williams and Don Drysdale ready to pitch. Drysdale was the Dodgers' ace and would go on to win the Cy Young Award that season. But Alston went over to Drysdale and told him, "I'm saving you to start Game 1 against the Yankees."

Duke Snider talked about it in the book, *True Blue*, by Steve Delsohn. "I'm sitting next to Drysdale on the bench," Snider said, "and I tell him, 'What are you sitting here for? Go tell Walt you'll warm up and pitch the ninth inning.'

"Drysdale talked to Alston and came back. I asked him what Alston said. He said, 'Walt said I'm pitching against the Yankees tomorrow in the World Series.' I said, 'If we don't win, there is no World Series.'"

Williams came in with the bases loaded, one out, and the Dodgers clinging to a 4–3 lead. Orlando Cepeda hit a sacrifice fly to right to tie the game. Williams intentionally walked Ed Bailey to load the bases again then walked Jim Davenport to give the Giants a 5–4 lead. They tacked on another run when second baseman Larry Burright made an error on Jose Pagan's grounder.

The Giants brought in Billy Pierce, who pitched so beautifully in Game 1, to finish it out, and he retired the Dodgers in order in the bottom of the ninth. But the fireworks were just beginning.

"It got ugly," Dodgers catcher John Roseboro said. "Drysdale had volunteered to go in, and Alston wanted to save him. So we were irate. And there was champagne in our clubhouse, there was whiskey, all the celebration stuff they couldn't get out. So you had a lot of players drinking and cussing. Then Alston went into his office and wouldn't come out. Guys were yelling, 'Come out, you gutless SOB.'"

So the 1962 season ended in anger. But 1963 would end in joy.

Sweeping the Yankees

The 1963 World Series put Sandy Koufax's name into the national consciousness and finally erased the stigma of the Yankees' dominance over the Dodgers through the years. Sure, the Brooklyn Dodgers beat the Yankees in the 1955 World Series, but they had lost to the Yankees in 1941, 1947, 1949, 1952, 1953, and 1956.

The Dodgers won the National League pennant by six games, finishing with a 99–63 record. Koufax won the Cy Young Award and the Most Valuable Player Award after going 25–5 with a 1.88 ERA and 306 strikeouts in 311 innings.

Game 1 was all Koufax as he struck out a World Series–record 15 Yankees in a 5–2 victory at Yankee Stadium, including striking out Yankees second baseman Bobby Richardson three times, the only time in his 1,448-game major league career that he struck out more than twice in a game. Clete Boyer was the only Yankee who did not strike out.

And can you imagine how they felt after hearing what Koufax said after the game?

"I felt a little weak," Koufax told the gathered reporters. "I just felt a little tired in general early in the game. Then I felt a little weak in the middle of the game. Then I got some of my strength back, but I was a little weak again at the end."

Really? He was weak and struck out 15 Yankees. How would he have done if he had felt okay?

Koufax went on to talk a little more about his general malaise.

"I lost my rhythm in the middle innings, probably because I was pitching too fast. And I got a little tired around the sixth and seventh. The fastball started coming back a little. After I got tired, I stopped throwing the curve so much. I was never worried about my control. The best thing about my pitching today was control."

Koufax ended the game by striking out Yankees pinch-hitter Harry Bright for his 15th K of the game, erasing former teammate Carl Erskine's

Sandy Koufax pitches in the early stages of Game 1 of the 1963 World Series at Yankee Stadium in the Bronx, New York, on October 2, 1963. Koufax struck out 15 Yankees for a new World Series record on the way to a 5–2 win. *(AP Photo)*

name from the top spot of the record book. Erskine had struck out 14 Yankees in the 1953 World Series.

"I thought to myself, *I'd like to get that 15th strikeout in the ninth*," Koufax said. "But my emotions were mixed on that some."

Yankees catcher Yogi Berra summed it up best after the game, "I wonder how come he lost five games this year."

Game 2 was a 4–1 Dodgers victory. Willie Davis doubled in two runs in the first inning, Bill "Moose" Skowron homered, and Tommy Davis had two triples to lead the Dodgers as Johnny Podres notched the win over Al Downing. It was a pedestrian performance for Podres, but only if you compared it to Koufax in Game 1. Podres gave up six hits and struck out four in 8⅓ innings.

Trailing 4–0, the Yankees finally broke through in the ninth when Hector Lopez doubled with one out. Alston replaced Podres with Ron Perranoski, who gave up a run-scoring single to Elston Howard before getting the last two outs.

Like Koufax after Game 1, Podres also downplayed his performance. "The Yankees hit a lot of balls real good. Mantle probably would have had three home runs today if we had been playing this game in Dodger Stadium. Mickey didn't get any hits off me, but he hit me real good."

Continuing the trend of not being boastful, Alston wasn't too impressed that his team was up 2–0 in the Series and heading home to Dodger Stadium.

"It don't mean a thing," Alston said, "if we don't win two more."

Game 3 sent defending Cy Young winner Don Drysdale to the mound against Jim Bouton, who would go on to claim greater fame as the author of *Ball Four*, one of the best baseball books ever written. And it turned into quite the pitcher's duel.

The Dodgers scored in the bottom of the first when Tommy Davis singled in Jim Gilliam. That concluded the scoring for the day as the Dodgers won 1–0 on a three-hit shutout by Drysdale, who struck out nine.

Following the footsteps of his teammates, Drysdale said it was no big deal. "I don't know if this was the best I've ever pitched, but I had real good stuff and I was able to put almost every pitch right where I wanted it to go," Drysdale said before praising his opponent.

"These Yankees are tremendous. I have a lot of respect for them, and I knew I would have to be good…and lucky, too."

Game 4 saw more of the same. The Dodgers scored in the fifth on a Frank Howard home run. The Yankees tied it on a Mickey Mantle home run in the top of the seventh. But in the bottom of the inning, Jim Gilliam hit a hopper to Yankees third baseman Clete Boyer who threw to first. First baseman Joe Pepitone lost track of the ball, which hit him in the arm and rolled down the right-field line, allowing Gilliam to make it all the way to third. He then scored on Willie Davis' sacrifice fly.

Koufax went all the way again, giving up one run and six hits while striking out eight. He was named Series MVP.

So just one year after the season ended in acrimony, with players cursing at him, Alston was able to smile.

"This makes up for everything," he said after the Game 4 win.

Lost somewhat in the shuffle was the fact that Howard's home run was the first hit into the second deck at Dodger Stadium.

"I just guessed right," Howard said. "I was looking for a breaking pitch, and that's what Whitey [Ford] threw. I thought it might curve foul, but then I knew it was a homer."

Koufax, the star of the Series, said he pitched better in Game 4 than when he struck out 15 in Game 1.

"I think I was a more consistent pitcher today," Koufax told the assembled media. "I thought I made my two best pitches in the ninth. You have to be fortunate to beat the Yankees, and I certainly was."

The Yankees, who thought winning the World Series was a birth-right for them, were disconsolate. "We'll take a razzing," said Ford, who lost Games 1 and 4. "We always do anyway. Whenever we do any little thing wrong, we hear it. Wherever we go, 99 percent of the people root against us."

Mickey Mantle said the 1963 loss was worse than the loss to the Pittsburgh Pirates in 1960 when Bill Mazeroski hit his memorable walk-off home run to end Game 7.

"You have to lose sometimes, but never four straight," Mantle said in the clubhouse after the Game 4 loss. "People forget what happened in Pittsburgh, but they'll never forget this. I know I won't."

Dodgers fans certainly didn't. In 2012, the 1963 World Series sweep of the Yankees was voted the third-greatest moment in Dodger Stadium history.

Big D

D on Drysdale was a lot of things to a lot of people. Cy Young winner. Hall of Famer. Intimidating brushback pitcher. Big game winner. Actor. Baseball broadcaster.

One man was there for pretty much every moment of Drysdale's career: Vin Scully. Drysdale not only pitched for the Dodgers, from 1956 to 1969 he was part of the Dodgers' broadcast team and again from 1988 until his death on July 3, 1993.

In an interview conducted in 2013, Scully noted the differences between Drysdale and Sandy Koufax.

"I think one of the things when you look back over the years, you had Don Drysdale and Sandy Koufax, and they were as different as left and right.

"Sandy was very quiet. If Sandy was going out to dinner with a player, it would be the third-string catcher or a backup infielder, and they would just go quietly and have dinner.

"Don was the Pied Piper. If Don was going to go out to dinner, he'd have six or seven players with him. Don had a magnetism about him. Sandy, the other players thought he was absolutely unbelievable. Don

23

was one of them. He was very outgoing, so there was no surprise that he would eventually go into broadcasting because that was his nature. He was a very happy-go-lucky guy, and the players loved to be with him because where he would go there would be fun, guaranteed. Party hats and noisemakers and all of that.

"But when he stepped on the field, he was a totally different person. He was a tremendous competitor who would not mind at all trying to frighten the hitter."

And who did Drysdale try to frighten the most with an inside pitch?

"I think Don tried to frighten Henry Aaron as much if not more than any other hitter. And I am pretty sure if you looked it up, Aaron had more home runs against him than any other pitcher."

Scully was right, of course. Aaron hit 17 home runs against Drysdale in his career. Second? Aaron hit nine off Robin Roberts.

Drysdale is known by many now as a pitcher who was willing to pitch inside, and if a batter showed him up by looking at a home run too long or digging in at the plate, you could bet he would get a fastball to the ribs in the next at-bat. Drysdale hit 154 batters in his career and led the league in hit batsmen from 1958 to 1961 and again in 1965.

In recent years, it seems a pitcher gets a warning if he even looks at a batter funny, so how would Drysdale adjust to today's game?

"He would not have adjusted," Scully said. "The hitters and umpires would have had to adjust to him. The only difference really, the rewards are so great today, that no one really wants to hit anyone else. Because they realize, 'If I hit this fella, they are definitely gonna hit me, and I'm making X million of dollars and I don't want to get hurt.' So I think that is a definite feeling among the players.

"But you still have to pitch inside. You must pitch inside. And you are going to hit people once in a while. And if the numbers pile up where you are constantly hitting people, you get a bad reputation.

Right-hander Don Drysdale (center), who pitched the Dodgers to a 7–2 win over the Minnesota Twins in Los Angeles to even the World Series at 2–2, gets a headlock on two Dodgers who smashed home runs on October 10, 1965—Lou Johnson (left) and Wes Parker (right). *(AP Photo)*

"Look at Ian Kennedy with Arizona [Kennedy had been involved in a couple of bench-clearing brawls in the 2013 season, one with the Dodgers]. Kennedy is probably a lovely guy. But he knows to make his money that he must pitch inside, and he's gonna hit a few people.

"Don would not have said, 'Well, I will bow to the wishes of the umpires.' No, he would have continued to pitch inside."

Perfection

In 1995, the Society for American Baseball research, a group filled with historians, statisticians, and those who love the game, was asked to pick the best-pitched game in Major League Baseball history. The result was the perfect game pitched by Sandy Koufax on September 9, 1965, against the Chicago Cubs at Dodger Stadium.

A quick capsule of that game looks like this:

First inning: Donald Young pops to second. Glenn Beckert and Billy Williams strike out looking.

Second inning: Ron Santo fouls to the catcher. Ernie Banks strikes out swinging. Byron Browne lines to center.

Third inning: Chris Krug flies to center. Don Kessinger flies to right. Bob Hendley strikes out looking.

Fourth inning: Young fouls to first. Beckert flies to right. Williams strikes out looking.

Fifth inning: Santo flies to left. Banks strikes out swinging. Browne grounds to short.

Sixth inning: Krug grounds to short. Kessinger grounds to third. Hendley strikes out swinging.

Seventh inning: Young strikes out swinging. Beckert flies to right. Williams flies to left.

Eighth inning: Santo strikes out looking. Banks and Browne strike out swinging.

Ninth inning: Krug strikes out swinging. Joey Amalfitano, batting for Kessinger, strikes out swinging. Harvey Kuenn, batting for Hendley, strikes out swinging.

27 batters, 27 outs, 14 by strikeout.

Of course, don't remind Bob Hendley, the Cubs' starter, of that. He probably pitched the best game in a losing effort in history, giving up only one hit in the game and losing 1–0 on an unearned run.

In the bottom of the fifth, Hendley walked Lou Johnson. Ron Fairly sacrificed. Johnson stole third and scored when Krug threw the ball over the third baseman's head.

The Dodgers' lone hit came in the bottom of the seventh, a double by Johnson.

"It's a shame Hendley had to get beat that way," Koufax said after the game. "But I'm glad we got the run or we might have been here all night."

Kuenn, a former batting champion, made the last out of the game. After the count on Kuenn went to 2–1, Kuenn swung at a pitch off the strike zone.

"I went for a bad pitch," Kuenn said. "But the last one was a strike. He was throwing. He was throwing real hard." Kuenn also made the last out in Koufax's 1963 no-hitter against the San Francisco Giants.

Amazingly, Dodger Stadium was only half full, as there were only 29,139 in attendance that night. Most people listened to the perfect game on the radio, and Vin Scully's call of the final inning has become oft-quoted by Dodgers fans even to this day.

The Dodgers were kind enough to provide a transcript of the ninth inning, which is reprinted here in its entirety for one of the few times since that day.

Three times in his sensational career has Sandy Koufax walked out to the mound to pitch a fateful ninth where he turned in a no-hitter. But tonight, September the 9th, nineteen hundred and sixty five, he made the toughest walk of his career, I'm sure, because through eight innings he has pitched a perfect game. He has struck out 11, he has retired 24 consecutive batters, and the first man he will look at is catcher Chris Krug, big right-hand hitter, flied to second, grounded to short. Dick Tracewski is now at second base and Koufax ready and delivers: curveball for a strike.

0 and one the count to Chris Krug. Out on deck to pinch-hit is one of the men we mentioned earlier as a possible, Joey Amalfitano. Here's the strike one pitch to Krug: fastball, swung on and missed, strike two. And you can almost taste the pressure now. Koufax lifted his cap, ran his fingers through his black hair, then pulled the cap back down, fussing at the bill. Krug must feel it too as he backs out, heaves a sigh, took off his helmet, put it back on and steps back up to the plate.

Tracewski is over to his right to fill up the middle, Kennedy is deep to guard the line. The strike two pitch on the way: fastball, outside, ball one. Krug started to go after it and held up, and Torborg held the ball high in the air trying to convince Vargo but Eddie said, 'No sir.' One and two the count to Chris Krug. It is 9:41 PM on September the 9th. The 1–2 pitch on the way: curveball, tapped foul off to the left of the plate.

The Dodgers defensively in this spine-tingling moment: Sandy Koufax and Jeff Torborg. The boys who will try and stop anything hit their way: Wes Parker, Dick Tracewski, Maury Wills, and John Kennedy; the outfield of Lou Johnson, Willie Davis, and Ron Fairly. And there's 29,000 people in the ballpark and a million butterflies. Twenty-nine thousand, one hundred and thirty-nine paid.

Koufax into his windup and the 1–2 pitch: fastball, fouled back out of play. In the Dodger dugout Al Ferrara gets up and walks down near the runway, and it begins to get tough to be a teammate and sit in the dugout and have to watch. Sandy back of the rubber, now toes it. All the boys in the bullpen straining to get a better look as they look through the wire fence in left field. One and two the count to Chris Krug. Koufax, feet together, now to his windup and the 1–2 pitch: fastball outside, ball two. [Crowd boos.]

A lot of people in the ballpark now are starting to see the pitches with their hearts. The pitch was outside, Torborg tried to pull it over the plate but Vargo, an experienced umpire, wouldn't go for it. Two and two the count to Chris Krug. Sandy reading signs, into his windup, 2–2 pitch: fastball, got him swingin'!

Sandy Koufax has struck out 12. He is two outs away from a perfect game.

Here is Joe Amalfitano to pinch-hit for Don Kessinger. Amalfitano is from Southern California, from San Pedro. He was an original bonus boy with the Giants. Joey's been around, and as we mentioned earlier, he has helped to beat the Dodgers twice, and on deck is Harvey Kuenn. Kennedy is tight to the bag at third, the fastball, a strike. 0 and one with one out in the ninth inning, one to nothing, Dodgers. Sandy reading, into his windup and the strike-one pitch: curveball, tapped foul, 0 and two. And Amalfitano walks away and shakes himself a little bit and swings the bat. And Koufax with a new ball, takes a hitch at his belt and walks behind the mound.

I would think that the mound at Dodger Stadium right now is the loneliest place in the world.

Sandy fussing, looks in to get his sign, 0 and two to Amalfitano. The strike two pitch to Joe: fastball, swung on and missed, strike three!

He is one out away from the promised land, and Harvey Kuenn is comin' up.

So Harvey Kuenn is batting for Bob Hendley. The time on the scoreboard is 9:44. The date, September the 9th, 1965, and Koufax working on veteran Harvey Kuenn. Sandy into his windup and the pitch, a fastball for a strike! He has struck out, by the way, five consecutive batters, and that's gone unnoticed. Sandy ready and the strike-one pitch: very high, and he lost his hat. He really forced that one. That's only the second time tonight where I have had the feeling that Sandy threw instead of pitched, trying to get that little extra, and that time he tried so hard his hat fell off—he took an extremely long stride to the plate—and Torborg had to go up to get it.

One and one to Harvey Kuenn. Now he's ready: fastball, high, ball two. You can't blame a man for pushing just a little bit now. Sandy backs off, mops his forehead, runs his left index finger along his forehead, dries it off on his left pants leg. All the while Kuenn just waiting. Now Sandy looks in. Into his windup and the 2–1 pitch to Kuenn: swung on and missed, strike two!

It is 9:46 PM.

Two and two to Harvey Kuenn, one strike away. Sandy into his windup, here's the pitch.

Swung on and missed, a perfect game!

[38 seconds of cheering.]

On the scoreboard in right field it is 9:46 PM in the City of the Angels, Los Angeles, California. And a crowd of 29,139 just sitting in to see the only pitcher in baseball history to hurl four no-hit, no-run games. He has done it four straight years, and now he caps it—on his fourth no-hitter he made it a perfect game. And Sandy Koufax, whose name will always remind you of strikeouts, did it with a flurry. He struck out the last six consecutive batters. So when he wrote his name in capital letters in the record books, that "K" stands out even more than the O-U-F-A-X.

That is why Vin Scully is the best broadcaster in sports history.

Roseboro vs. Marichal

It was a day no one in attendance would ever forget—the day Giants pitcher Juan Marichal almost killed Dodgers catcher John Roseboro with a baseball bat.

The August 22, 1965, game between the Giants and the Dodgers seemed like any other. The Dodgers scored in the first inning when Ron Fairly doubled home Maury Wills, who had opened the game with a single.

The first sign of trouble came in the second inning. Marichal threw a couple of pitches up and in, knocking Wills off his feet both times. The Dodgers' dugout had a few choice words, better left unprinted in a family book, before Wills lined to second. In the third inning, Fairly came to bat, and he tasted the dirt a couple of times after Marichal threw at him.

That brings us to the bottom of the third, with Marichal leading off. And before the inning started, Dodgers starter Sandy Koufax was given one command—throw at Juan Marichal.

There was one problem, however. Koufax didn't always have the best control, so he was afraid that if he threw at Marichal, he might hit him in the head and kill him. So an alternate plan was made. Koufax threw a strike, and then threw one high and inside. Marichal glared at him, and that is when the new plan went into effect. Roseboro threw the ball back to Koufax but threw it as hard as he could right past Marichal's head and, according to Marichal, actually nicking him in the ear. At that point, Marichal turned and said something to Roseboro.

In an interview with the *San Francisco Chronicle* after the game, Giants manager Herm Franks said Marichal asked Roseboro, "Why did you do that?"

Roseboro took one step toward Marichal, who swung his bat and hit Roseboro in the head. Blood started spurting everywhere as players from both teams ran toward home plate.

The enraged Dodgers were trying to get at Marichal, and the stunned Giants were trying to protect their teammate when one man walked over to Roseboro, who by this time wanted a piece of Marichal himself.

"John, they put your eye out," Willie Mays said to Roseboro. Manager Walt Alston and several other players were convinced Marichal had knocked Roseboro's eye out, since the space where his left eye would be was covered in blood.

Mays walked Roseboro off the field and into the Dodgers clubhouse as the Giants hustled Marichal into their clubhouse. Players on both teams credited Mays, probably the most respected player in baseball at that point, with preventing things from escalating into a full-fledged riot.

Roseboro suffered a 2" gash in the hairline just above his forehead. Blood from the gash streamed down into his left eye, which was uninjured.

Dodgers trainer Bill Buhler said Roseboro "had a knot in the middle of his skull that would take your whole hand to cover.

The next day, both Roseboro and Marichal released statements.

Roseboro's statement: "People ask me what kind of punishment Marichal should receive. I'll tell you: He and I in a room together for about 10 minutes.

"When I threw the ball back to Koufax, Marichal told me I'd better not hit him with the ball. I certainly was close enough to hit him had I wanted to, but the ball didn't touch him.

"I took a step toward Marichal, and that's when he began swinging the bat against my head. I don't know how many times he hit me because I don't remember much of what happened after his first swing. I was just trying to grab that bat.

"I do remember Willie Mays telling me my left eye was bleeding and wiping my face. My eye was full of blood but it wasn't cut. Later on in the game, Mays came into our clubhouse to find out how I was.

"I'm not a great fan of Marichal. In fact, we're unfriendly."

Marichal's statement: "First of all, I want to apologize for hitting Roseboro with my bat. I am sorry I did that. But he was coming toward me, with his mask in his hand, and I was afraid he was going to hit me with his mask, so I swung my bat. If he had only said something, I would not have swung. I hit him once, and I am sorry.

"I think the anger started on Friday night. On his [next to] last time at bat in that game, Maury Wills was awarded first base for catcher's interference. Our team thought Wills deliberately stepped back, forcing Tom Haller to tip Wills' bat with his glove. So when Matty Alou came to bat in the next inning, he did the same thing, but the plate umpire, [Al Forman], did not award him first base. Then Roseboro yelled over at our dugout, 'If this stuff keeps up, we're going to get one of you guys and get him good—right in the ear.' The umpire must have heard this. And later, Roseboro repeated it to Orlando Cepeda. That is why I want him present when I meet Warren Giles.

"When I came to bat on Sunday, the first pitch was a perfect strike. The second one was a little inside. Johnny Roseboro deliberately dropped the ball so he could get behind me. Then he threw the ball back to Koufax real hard—nobody ever throws the ball back to the pitcher that hard—and it ticked my ear. I might expect Koufax to throw at me, but I did not look for someone to throw at me from behind me. Then I turn around and I say, 'Why did you do that?' He did not say a word. He just took off his mask and came toward me. I was afraid he was going to hit me with his mask, so I hit him with my bat. I am sorry but many times our players on the Giants are hit by pitches and sometimes hurt, and nobody says anything then."

Now imagine something like this happening in the current game. How big a suspension do you think Marichal would get? Fifty games? One hundred?

Marichal was suspended for eight playing dates and fined $1,750.

Roseboro missed two games because of his injury. He sued Marichal after the season for $110,000 in damages. The case was settled in 1970, with the financial terms undisclosed, but they were rumored to be about $7,500.

Years after the incident, Marichal and Roseboro would appear at old-timer's games together, and while neither man explained exactly how the ice was broken, the fact was that they became friends.

Roseboro campaigned for Marichal to be elected to the Hall of Fame because some writers said they would not vote for Marichal because of the bat incident. Marichal was elected in 1983, in his third year of eligibility, and the first person he thanked was John Roseboro.

"There were no hard feelings on my part, and I thought if that was made public, people would believe that this was really over with," Roseboro said in an interview with the *Los Angeles Times* in 1983. "So I saw him at a Dodger old-timers' game and we posed for pictures together and I actually visited him in the Dominican. The next year, he was in the Hall of Fame.

"Hey, over the years you learn to forget things."

John Roseboro died in 2002. Juan Marichal was a pallbearer and a speaker at his funeral, where he said, "One of the great events of my life was John Roseboro forgiving me. It takes special people to forgive."

Champions Again

The 1965 World Series between the Dodgers and the Minnesota Twins was supposed to be a mere formality. There were three things certain then—death, taxes, and the Dodgers sweeping the Twins in the World Series. After all, the Dodgers had won two World Series in the last six years, and this was Minnesota's first appearance in a World Series.

But somebody forgot to tell the Twins.

Game 1 was rout—for the Twins. They scored six runs in the third inning off Don Drysdale on their way to an 8–2 victory. But the Dodgers had Sandy Koufax starting Game 2, so all would be okay, right?

"I've made the statement that Koufax is the only pitcher I'd pay to watch when he's just warming up," Twins manager Sam Mele said on the eve of Game 2. "We know Sandy is a real good one. But we're going to try to get hits and play the same game we did today."

It was 50 degrees when the game started, but the Twins and starting pitcher Jim Kaat warmed up quickly, defeating the Dodgers and Koufax 5–1 to take a 2–0 Series lead.

"No, the cold weather didn't bother me," Koufax said. "I pitched and had good stuff on colder days. I knew what I wanted to do out there, I just couldn't do it. Kaat and Minnesota just did a better job."

But the Series returned to Dodger Stadium for Games 3, 4, and 5, and that's when things turned around.

Claude Osteen went all the way for the Dodgers in Game 3, pitching a five-hit shutout in a 4–0 victory. Drysdale returned to form in Game 4, striking out 11 Twins in a 5–2 victory. Koufax struck out 10 and gave up only four hits in a 6–0 victory in Game 5, and suddenly the Dodgers had a 3–2 Series lead. Unfortunately, there were no more games left at Dodger Stadium.

Game 6 was the Jim "Mudcat" Grant show. Grant not only pitched a great game, limiting the Dodgers to one run and six hits, he also hit a three-run home run as the Twins won 5–1 to force a decisive Game 7.

This left Dodgers manager Walt Alston with a quandary. Who should start Game 7? Drysdale on three days rest, or Koufax on two?

"It will either be Sandy Koufax or Don Drysdale tomorrow," Alston said after the Game 6 loss. "I won't decide until morning, maybe not until game time, because I want to think about it."

Koufax wanted everyone to know that he was ready. "I feel good. My arm feels good. There's nothing to save my arm for after tomorrow. If I'm asked to pitch, I'm not going out there to lose."

Drysdale, on the other hand, was a little sore. "My hand was a little numb pitching in the ninth in Game 4, but it's okay, just a little tingling sensation at times."

So who would you have chosen to pitch Game 7?

Alston went with Koufax, but he had Drysdale warming up in the bullpen in the first couple of innings, just in case.

Drysdale needn't have bothered.

In one of the most amazing pitching performances of all time, pitching on two days rest in Game 7 of the World Series, Sandy Koufax struck out 10 Twins, including the last two batters of the game, and gave up only three hits as the Dodgers won the game 2–0 and the World Series.

What made Koufax's performance even more amazing is that his arm was hurting so much, he couldn't control his curveball. So he threw nothing but fastballs from the third inning on.

"I didn't have a curve ball at all," Koufax said after Game 7. "When I threw it I couldn't get it over. And those first few innings I really didn't know how long I was going to last.

"Then I seemed to get my second wind. In the last three, the fastball seemed to move better, and I got stronger."

Paul Zimmerman, then with the *Los Angeles Times*, asked Koufax if he ever had other days when he had to rely exclusively on the fastball.

"Yes, but if I had a choice I'd rather not have it happen in a World Series, like it did to me today.

"I was worried in the fifth and again in the sixth when I seemed to lose my rhythm. When Walt came out to talk to me, he told me not to try and get anything extra on the ball, just pitch to spots."

And with that, Koufax cemented his legacy. Or, as Drysdale said to him during the celebration after Game 7, "You beautiful, beautiful fellow."

Little did anyone know it would be Koufax's last World Series victory, or that he only had one more season left in his amazing career.

Koufax Retires

The Dodgers returned to the World Series in 1966 but were swept by the Baltimore Orioles. Sandy Koufax lost Game 2 of that Series. Although the Dodgers were swept, fans looked forward to the future because the team had the best pitcher in baseball on its side. Koufax went 27–9 in 1966, and the rest of his numbers were staggering: 41 starts, 27 complete games, 323 innings pitched, 317 strikeouts, and a 1.73 ERA. He was a unanimous choice for the Cy Young Award and finished second in MVP voting to Roberto Clemente. In four years, he had won three Cy Young Awards, one MVP Award, and finished second in MVP voting two other times.

He was also only 30 years old, so the Dodgers could look forward to at least five more years of Koufax on top of his game, right?

Wrong. The pain in Koufax's elbow was too much for him to bear any longer, and doctors told him he could lose the use of the arm if he continued to pitch, so Koufax became one of the few people to walk away at the top of his game, never to return.

At the news conference announcing his retirement, Koufax explained his decision.

"I've had a few too many shots and taken a few too many pills. I don't want to take the chance of completely disabling myself.

"The decision was based partly on medical advice and partly on my own feeling. It got to the point where I was told I could do permanent damage. I had a couple of doctors talk to me about it.

"My health is something that means too much to me. I decided I had a lot of years left after baseball, and I want to live them with the full use of my body. I had to take a shot every ball game. That's more than I wanted to do. I had stomach aches from the pain pills. I'd be high half the time [in] my ball games from the pills. I don't want that.

"The pain had become more continual. I think I had one ball game last season when the arm didn't hurt me. The arthritis is going to get worse as I get older. I hope this will slow it down. The thing that caused it is the irritation, and the irritation is growing. I have to hope that by not irritating it further, I will help slow it down. Arms aren't made for what pitchers ask it to do."

The big surprise at the news conference was the fact that not one Dodgers front-office person attended. Team owner Walter O'Malley was on a trip to Japan, and GM Buzzie Bavasi had asked Koufax to delay announcing his retirement until after O'Malley returned. Koufax agreed then changed his mind.

"He said to me, 'Will you call a press conference for Friday'" Bavasi said. "I said, 'No, I think we owe Walter O'Malley of waiting till he returned from Japan.' Then we decided we would announce it after that.

"But Thursday night Sandy called me and said he'd made up his mind to announce it right away. He said he was definitely going through with it Friday. I wished him luck and said I could have no part of it."

When O'Malley returned from Japan, he released the following statement on behalf of the team:

"We wish Sandy great happiness and good health in retirement. He leaves a record of performance in baseball that might not again be equaled.

"How many more records he might have established is now only a matter of conjecture. We respect his decision and wish him only the best. He was the best."

Many people today don't realize just how much pain Koufax was in. Today, he could have had arthroscopic surgery and missed a couple of months, only to come back good as new. But not in 1966.

After each start, Koufax soaked his left elbow in ice water for 45 minutes. He received cortisone shots every other day during the 1966 season, and he took the pain reliever called Butazolidin before and during games. Butazolidin was banned in the 1970s because it can cause irreversible liver degradation.

Between starts, the pain in his arm was so bad that he had to comb his hair and shave with his right hand.

But the Dodgers could survive the loss of Koufax, couldn't they? After all, they still had Drysdale, and could losing one player really kill a team that had been in three of the last four World Series?

After finishing first in 1965 and 1966, the Dodgers sank to eighth in 1967 with a 73–89 record. They finished seventh in 1968. They wouldn't reach the World Series again until 1974, and they wouldn't win it again until 1981. That was the value of Sandy Koufax.

CHAPTER 3
THE 1970s

The Singer Throwin' Machine

Great things were expected of pitcher Bill Singer in 1970. He was coming off a season in which he had made the All-Star Game and had won 20 games. He was penciled in as the Dodgers' No. 2 starter and, at age 26, figured to be a mainstay for years to come.

Singer pitched a shutout in his second start of the season but felt really tired after the game. That fatigue lingered into his next start against the Cincinnati Reds, where he gave up four runs in four innings and had to come out of the game.

Trying to find a reason for his lethargy, doctors ran some tests and came back with some bad news—Singer had hepatitis. He was immediately checked into a hospital, where he was given fluids and medication. Singer was in the hospital for three weeks then ordered to get complete bed rest at home for the next three weeks.

After his start against Cincinnati, Singer didn't even pick up a baseball until the first week of June. The Dodgers didn't put him back on the active roster until June 14.

Singer only lasted two innings in his return to the rotation and then had four strong starts mixed with a couple of poor starts. Still, he was on a relatively short leash when he went into his start against the Philadelphia Phillies on July 20 at Dodger Stadium.

Twenty-seven outs later, Singer had his first no-hitter. When the last out, a foul out by Byron Browne, was made, Singer sank to his knees in relief, joy, and exhaustion.

"It's a miracle," Singer said. "I'm so happy, I could cry. The tears are there."

The only scary moment came in the seventh inning when the Phillies' Don Money hit a grounder to the right of Singer, whose throw to first pulled first baseman Wes Parker off the bag just as Money arrived.

Seeing that his throw was not on the money, the official scorer gave Singer an error, preserving the no-hitter.

"I was hoping it would be called an error," Singer said. "But the fact is I did make a number of mistakes on the play. I underestimated Money's speed, and I threw hurriedly. If I'd kept my cool, I would have gotten him easily."

Just to illustrate how much baseball has changed, after the game, team owner Walter O'Malley gave Singer a bonus of $500 for pitching the no- hitter.

Tradition says that the pitcher in a no-hitter will find a bottle of champagne in his locker in the clubhouse when he returns there after the game. Knowing Singer couldn't drink alcohol, his teammates helped themselves to the champagne, but left Singer a replacement—a pitcher of iced tea.

Jackie, Roy, and Sandy

It's hard to get your uniform number retired if you played for the Dodgers. A lot of greats have never had their numbers permanently withheld, including Fernando Valenzuela, Steve Garvey, Ron Cey, Don Newcombe, and Orel Hershiser. Not even Lance Rautzhan—okay, I'm kidding about that last one, but I promised myself I'd work the name of my favorite Dodger when I was a kid into the book, and this was the perfect spot.

The Brooklyn Dodgers never retired any numbers and neither had the team when it moved to L.A.—until it decided to retire three numbers on June 4, 1972. And what a trio of names associated with those numbers: Jackie Robinson (42), Roy Campanella (39), and Sandy Koufax (32).

The Dodgers retired their numbers on Old-Timer's Day at Dodger Stadium, so a host of Hall of Famers and other great baseball players were on hand to see it happen. Former Yankees manager Casey Stengel said a few words. So did former Yankees great Mickey Mantle. Joe DiMaggio was there, as was Newcombe.

Those legendary names and more surrounded home plate as Campanella, Robinson, and Koufax made their way to home plate for the ceremony. With a capacity crowd there early, each man took his turn to speak.

"Growing up in Brooklyn," Koufax said, "my heroes were Roy Campanella and Jackie Robinson. I never thought I would be standing here with them today."

Robinson spoke next. "This is one of the truly great moments of my life. I'm grateful for everything that has happened."

Finally, Campanella spoke, "It is indeed a pleasure to return to L.A. I am only sorry that I didn't get to play one game in L.A. But I'm still a Dodger, and I always will be."

It was Robinson's first visit to Dodger Stadium in several years. He had a falling out with the club when they traded him to the Giants (Robinson retired instead of playing for the Dodgers' main rivals) and when Walter O'Malley and Branch Rickey, the man who signed Robinson to the Dodgers and helped protect him, became enemies.

In fact, Robinson had refused to come to see his number be retired until he had a meeting with team president Peter O'Malley two days before the ceremony.

"As my way of protest," Robinson said, "I stopped going to Old-Timer's games. If it hadn't been for the good feeling I had for Don Newcombe, I doubt very much I would have come today. Baseball and Jackie Robinson haven't had much to say to each other. I told Peter I was disturbed at the way baseball treats its black players after their playing days are through.

"I was very impressed with Peter's attitude. I don't know what he can do about it, but at least he has a sensitivity to it."

Robinson, who had just turned 53, was in poor health. He had a heart attack the year before and had diabetes. On the day his number was retired, he spoke optimistically about his health.

"Health is a progressive thing, but I've felt a lot better in the last four or five months. One looks at himself, at how things turn out, and I'm pleased about what's happening on the playing field.

"But although we can talk about it, I don't think we'll see a black manager in my lifetime."

Robinson was right. He died on October 24, a little more than four months after his number was retired. The first black manager arrived in 1975, when Frank Robinson was hired to manage the Cleveland Indians.

In 1997, on the 50th anniversary of Robinson breaking the color barrier, Major League Baseball announced that No. 42 would be retired by all teams, never to be worn again.

The Infield

In this era of free agency, finding one player who has spent 10 years with one team is nearly improbable. Finding an entire infield that has done that? Impossible.

Go online and find the Dodgers box score for June 13, 1973. Go ahead and find it now and print it out, the rest of us will wait here for you…

Got it? You may notice that the Dodgers lost to the Philadelphia Phillies 16–3. You may notice that pitchers Tommy John and Charlie Hough each gave up eight runs. But look at the list of batters. Steve Garvey played first base. Davey Lopes played second base. Bill Russell was the shortstop. And Ron Cey was at third base.

That date—June 13, 1973—is the date of the first game those four played the infield together. They would play together in almost every game until the end of the 1981 season. It is the longest-running infield in baseball history. They won four division titles, four National League pennants, and one World Series.

45

None of them are in the Hall of Fame, though you can make a case for Garvey and Cey. None of them have had their numbers retired by the team, which is a real shame.

It wasn't all smooth sailing. The four didn't always get along, and some of them resented Garvey for his All-American image and the attention he received, and cultivated, from the media.

Russell reached the majors first in April 1969, but not as a shortstop, as an outfielder. Garvey came to the majors in September 1969, but not as a first baseman, as a third baseman. Russell didn't hit well enough to play the outfield, so they put him at shortstop. Garvey had no arm at all and was the worst fielding third baseman in the majors, so they sent him to first base.

Cey came to the majors in 1971 as a third baseman and was pretty much the guy who forced Garvey off third and over to first. Lopes was also an outfielder at first, but the Dodgers needed a second baseman, so they had him play that position in the minors for a while before bringing him to the majors in 1972.

Ten days after first appearing in a box score together, Garvey, Lopes, Russell, and Cey started their first game together. It was the first of 833 games the foursome started. They combined for 21 All-Star selections and five Gold Gloves. The team changed around them, but from 1973 to 1981, you knew that when you went to a Dodgers game, you were going to see those four in the lineup.

They finally broke through and won a World Series in 1981, and that proved to be the quartet's last hurrah. Lopes was traded to the Oakland A's after the season. Garvey and Cey went the following year. Russell retired as a Dodger in 1986.

In 2013, the four reflected on their time together and the changes in baseball and to the Dodgers.

"What people want is a reminder of what it was like," Cey said. "The more you can see past successes of the team, it gives the fans hope. When you're in the moment, you don't reflect. But can you imagine what it would be like for the Dodgers to go to the World Series in this era four times in eight years? This city would be turned upside down."

But playing together for so long had its drawbacks. "We respected each other and knew each other's ability," Russell said. "You knew all the intimate stuff, some of the stuff you probably shouldn't know."

Lopes said they get along better now than they ever did. "I'm extremely proud of what they brought into my life and, hopefully, I've brought something into their lives. And that we can say, as a group, we lasted and accomplished something that no one in the game has come close to accomplishing again."

Steve Garvey, All-Star

Steve Garvey played so well in the last few weeks of the 1973 season that manager Walter Alston decided Garvey would be the regular first base in 1974. One problem, however, was that no one told the people who come up with the All-Star ballots. Garvey's name wasn't on it.

Garvey got off to a hot start, hitting .321 in April and .350 in May, and he quickly became the darling of Dodgers fans. He came out before games to sign autographs, and it seemed he wouldn't get in his car to drive home after games until he had spoken to every fan hanging around outside the team parking area.

Back in those days, there was only one way to vote for players—ushers at the stadiums around baseball would hand out actual ballots, and you would punch out the chad next to the person you wanted to vote for. Of course, without a spot on the ballot, you couldn't punch out a chad next to Garvey's name.

There was one solution to that problem. At the bottom of every ballot was a section where you could fill in the name and position of a player. Most people didn't pay attention to that because who wanted to take the time to write down someone's name when you could just punch a chad and be done with it?

Dodger fans, that's who.

Fans organized a write-in campaign to get Garvey voted to the All-Star team. Dodgers fans would grab stacks of ballots from ushers, fill out Garvey's name at the bottom, and return them without even bothering to pick any other starters.

It all paid off when Garvey was announced as the winner of the balloting at first base, receiving 1,082,489 votes, edging out Cincinnati's Tony Perez by about 50,000 votes.

And Garvey wouldn't be going alone, he would be joined by fellow starters Ron Cey and Jimmy Wynn, who won the balloting in the traditional way at third base and the outfield, respectively.

Garvey rewarded the fans' hard work by being named the MVP of the game after getting a single, a double, an RBI, and a run scored in the NL's 7–2 victory.

"I can't express in words themselves my thanks to the people who got me here," Garvey said while accepting the MVP trophy. "It's not my trophy, it's theirs."

Garvey went on to help lead the Dodgers to the World Series that season and was named National League MVP after the season ended.

The Catch and the Throw

The 1974 Dodgers defeated the Pittsburgh Pirates in the National League Championship Series and faced the mighty Oakland A's, the two-time defending World Series champion. And it was over quickly with the A's winning in five games.

But there is one highlight from the Series that Dodgers fans still talk about today.

Center fielder Jimmy Wynn was a key member of the '74 Dodgers, hitting .271 with 32 homers and 108 RBIs. Usually a standout defender, Wynn hurt his right shoulder making a diving catch near the end of the season, and after that his throwing arm had all the strength of a wet paper towel.

Knowing this, right fielder Joe Ferguson and Wynn had a deal. If a ball was hit between them and a runner was on third, Ferguson would make the catch with the hope that his stronger arm would hold the runner, or that he could throw them out trying to score.

Game 1 of the World Series reached the eighth inning and Oakland was leading 3–1. With Sal Bando on third for the A's, Reggie Jackson hit a fly ball to right center. With a left-hander up, Wynn was playing toward right-center and Ferguson was closer to the right-field line, so it looked like Wynn's ball all the way.

Wynn set himself for the catch, when at the last second Ferguson, who started racing over as soon as the ball was hit, cut in front of him, made the catch, and threw a perfect strike to catcher Steve Yeager 300' away. Bando barreled over Yeager, who held onto the ball for the out.

"I've made throws like that before, but there aren't too many opportunities," Ferguson said afterward.

Some Dodgers fans, even now, think Ferguson was just trying to show up Wynn, which isn't true.

"I called to him that I could take it and he said, 'Go ahead,'" Ferguson said.

Asked if that was true, Wynn responded, "Yep. Wasn't that one tremendous throw? It hurt my arm just to look at it."

The throw didn't help the Dodgers win, though, as they still lost the game 3–2. Ferguson made the last out with a man on first, which took a little of the thrill off one of the best throws in World Series history.

"It would have been more pleasant to have a hit," Ferguson said.

Monday Saves the Flag

The year 1976 was a turbulent time. Watergate was barely in the rearview mirror, thousands of Vietnam veterans were adjusting to life back home, and U.S. citizens were trying to decide whether to vote for Gerald Ford or Jimmy Carter as president.

As a backdrop to all of this, 1976 was also the year of our nation's Bicentennial, so most Americans had the duality of "I love my country/ What's going on with my country?" raging inside them.

On April 25, Rick Monday was playing center field for the Chicago Cubs against the Dodgers at Dodger Stadium. At one point during the game, two men ran onto the field and...well, let's allow Monday to recount the moment in his own words:

> In between the top and bottom of the fourth inning, I was just getting loose in the outfield, throwing the ball back and forth. Jose Cardenal was in left field, and I was in center. I don't know if I heard the crowd first or saw the guys first, but two people ran on the field. After a number of years of playing, when someone comes on the field, you don't know what's going to happen. Is it because they had too much to drink? Is it because they're trying to win a bet? Is it because they don't like you or do they have a message that they're trying to present?
>
> When these two guys ran on the field, something wasn't right. And it wasn't right from the standpoint that one of them had something cradled under his arm. It turned out to be an American flag. They came from the left-field corner, went past Cardenal to shallow left-center field.
>
> That's when I saw the flag. They unfurled it as if it was a picnic blanket. They knelt beside it, not to pay homage but to harm it as one of the guys was pulling out of his pocket some-where a big can of lighter fluid. He began to douse it.

What they were doing was wrong then, in 1976. In my mind, it's wrong now. It's the way I was raised. My thoughts were reinforced with my six years in the Marine Corps Reserves. It was also reinforced by a lot of friends who lost their lives protecting the rights and freedoms that flag represented.

So I started to run after them. To this day, I couldn't tell you what was running through my mind except I was mad, I was angry, and it was wrong for a lot of reasons.

Then the wind blew the first match out. There was hardly ever any wind at Dodger Stadium. The second match was lit just as I got there. I did think that if I could bowl them over, they can't do what they're trying to do.

I saw them go and put the match down to the flag. It's soaked in lighter fluid at this time. Well, they can't light it if they don't have it. So I just scooped it up.

My first thought was, *Is this on fire?* Well, fortunately, it was not. I continue to run. One of the men threw the can of lighter fluid at me. We found out he was not a prospect. He did not have a good arm. Thank goodness.

After the guys left, there was a buzz in the stands, people being aghast with what had taken place. Without being prompted, and I don't know where it started, but people began to sing 'God Bless America.' When I reflect back upon it now, I still get goose bumps.

But what was it like to be there as a fan? There is a famous photograph of Monday saving the flag, and if you look closely, you will see Ozzie Barrero, who was there that day and was kind enough to share his memories.

In James Roark's iconic photograph, I'm sitting in the front row of the left-field pavilion, farthest to the left [with dark hair,

51

white T-shirt and, like everyone else, a perplexed look]. When the two men jumped over the field box railing and ran onto the outfield grass waving the American flag, at first I thought perhaps they were trying to get on camera since the game was being broadcast back to Chicago that Sunday. But since it was between innings, when they knelt down in left center field and began fumbling with matches, I realized what they were actually attempting to do. At that point I remember wondering why there were no security personnel going after them.

My friends—all of whom are also in the photo sitting in the front row—and I used to attend as many Dodgers games as we could afford. Since we were just a bunch of Rosemead teenagers of modest means, the left-field pavilion was always our section of choice. Ironically, the 'cheap seats' turned out to be the prime viewing location for one of the most important sports-related moments in our nation's history.

As the whole incident unfolded, it truly appeared to be occurring in slow motion. When Monday began his full-speed sprint to save the flag, I had this bizarre feeling of being half a stride ahead of him and knowing that he was about to complete an incredibly brave and unselfish act. From my vantage point, I felt I was watching a surreal, one-act play from backstage. After all, it was happening in fan-friendly Dodger Stadium on a beautiful spring afternoon, during a routine warm-up in the middle of a game between two storied franchises. In that setting, the last thing anyone expected was a political protest. As it turned out, Monday's effort that day was perhaps the most patriotic 40-yard sprint an American athlete has ever run.

Ironically, I think most baseball fans remember it as a great moment in Dodgers history although Monday was a feared opponent and an All-Star center fielder for the Cubs at the

time. It was fitting that he made his way to the Dodgers organization the following year [and thank goodness for that or else
the 1981 championship would now be part of another team's
history].

Of course, the passing of time has served to only deepen my
appreciation of the moment, and I feel very fortunate to have
seen it in person. That day, Rick Monday, a successful professional athlete, did a very unusual thing—he instinctively risked
his safety [after all, no one really knew what those guys would
do] for something that had nothing to do with his personal or
professional advancement. It was a dramatic incident that tran-
scended the world of sports. In the aftermath of Vietnam and
the turmoil of the mid-1970s, Monday's saving of the flag in
1976 elevated our national pride and unified Americans of all
political and social backgrounds, if just for a brief moment.
But for those of my generation, this event has stood the test of
time and is seen as one of the sporting world's contributions to
American patriotism and our public spirit. In fact, one could
argue that there is only one other sporting event in the last
fifty years that has inspired and rallied our country more than
Monday's moment—the 'Miracle on Ice' in 1980.

Finally, I'm sure that millions from my generation remember the incessant 'Bicentennial minutes' [those little historical
anecdotes between shows] that ran on television for two full
years leading up to our country's 200-year celebration in 1976.
Put those thousands of minutes together, and they would never
come close to having the impact that Rick Monday had when he
saved the American flag from being burned on April 25, 1976.
It was the purest and most powerful example of a Bicentennial
minute that this country experienced at the time, and I'm grateful to be able to say that I was there to witness it.

Later that year, Monday was presented with the flag by the Dodgers, who traded for him during the off-season. He still has it hanging in his home.

Alston Retires

Walter Alston started managing the Dodgers in 1954 and chugged along for the next 22 years. He had won seven NL pennants (1955, 1956, 1959, 1963, 1965, 1966, 1974) and four World Series titles (1955, 1959, 1963, 1965), three of them in Los Angeles. Then Alston woke up on September 27, 1976, and decided it was time to retire.

"I don't suppose that my retirement will hit me until next spring or next summer," Alston said at his retirement news conference. "I've thought about taking this step at various times but not seriously until the last three or four days. When I woke up this morning, I knew it was the right time. I simply feel that I've been at it long enough, that it's time to let someone else take charge. I'm proud. I'm happy. I'm thankful about what I've been able to accomplish. The numbers aren't as important as the fact that I feel I've done the best possible job every day.

"Naturally, I feel a certain sadness. I'm also relieved in the sense that I now can do what I please. I can get away now to ride my motorcycle and my horses. To shoot pool and skeet, and to play a little golf."

His players were sad to see him go.

"Walt is the only guy I've ever known more stubborn than myself," Don Sutton said. "We've disagreed strongly, and in most cases he has been right. He's consistent, he's honest, he's upfront. I'm very disappointed that he is retiring."

"It's a sad day," Steve Garvey said. "To me, Walt has always represented the standard of his profession. He's been a man's manager. Not too many rules, not too many restrictions. All he expects is your honesty, your respect, a full effort. I feel blessed to have played for him."

A smiling Walter Alston told newsmen before the September 27, 1976, Dodgers game in Los Angeles that he wouldn't be back as manager after the season. He was 64 and the dean of major league baseball managers after 23 years as skipper. *(AP Photo)*

Alston was named NL manager of the year six times before retiring with a final record of 2,040–1,613. He had his number (24) retired by the team in 1977, and he was elected to the Baseball Hall of Fame in 1983.

Alston died at the age of 72 on October 1, 1984.

A great Walter Alston story, recounted in many books on the Dodgers, happened during the time when baseball teams still traveled by bus. One time the bus they used was old and had no air conditioning. Several Dodgers players spent the bus trip yelling and getting on Lee Scott, the club's traveling secretary.

Alston, sitting in the front of the bus, stood up and said, "I don't want to hear another word about this bus. And if anyone has something more to say about it, he can step off right now, and we'll settle it right here." No one said a word after that.

One of the amazing things about Alston's tenure with the team—he never had a multiyear contract. Each off-season, he would sign a one-year deal. He did that for 22 years.

Legendary *Los Angeles Times* columnist Jim Murray wrote the following when Alston retired: "I don't know whether you're Republican or Democrat or Catholic or Protestant, and I've known you for 18 years. You were as Middle-Western as a pitchfork. Black players who have a sure instinct for the closet bigot recognized immediately you didn't know what prejudice was. There was no 'side' to Walter Alston. What you saw was what you got."

Tommy Takes Charge

With Alston out, who would manage the Dodgers?

There were really only two candidates for the job, third-base coach Tommy Lasorda and first-base coach Jim Gilliam. Both men were supremely qualified, but Lasorda had one edge. Most of the players on the roster were young and had come up through the Dodgers' minor-league system. Their last stop in the minors was at Triple-A Albuquerque, which had been managed by Lasorda before he became a Dodgers coach in 1973. Of the current roster, the entire infield of Garvey, Lopes, Russell, and Cey, along with catcher Steve Yeager, had all come up under Lasorda's tutelage. That proved to be an important edge, though both men wanted the job badly.

"Sure, I would like to become the Dodgers' manager, but then, so would a lot of other people," Lasorda said the day Alston retired. "Would I be disappointed if it went to someone else? That's a hypothetical question that I can't answer."

Gilliam had been with the Dodgers since their days in Brooklyn, and he was equally hopeful about landing the job.

"Do I want to manage? Yes, of course! The O'Malleys know where to find me."

Three days after Alston retired, the Dodgers named Lasorda as his replacement.

Lasorda had been with the Dodgers since 1949, starting out as a pitcher and working his way up the ranks from scout, to minor-league manager, to coach. He won five pennants in his seven seasons as a minor-league manager.

The always-emotional Lasorda was in tears at the news conference an- nouncing he would be manager.

"I think that when someone wakes up and finds that when he has inherited a position vacated by the greatest manager in baseball history, it's like waking up to find you have inherited the Hope Diamond.

"I have been very loyal to this organization that I love so dearly. Loyalty is a two-way street, and this morning they showed me how much they love me."

While announcing Lasorda's promotion, the Dodgers also announced that Gilliam would return as first-base coach.

Lasorda's first order of business? Making sure he lined up a special guest to sing the National Anthem at the 1977 home opener—a fellow Italian who promised Lasorda that he would do it if he was ever named manager.

Sinatra Sings the Anthem

Former Dodgers manager Leo Durocher introduced Frank Sinatra to Tommy Lasorda in 1973. Lasorda recounts the meeting in his book, *The Artful Dodger*.

"I was brought in to meet him at a restaurant in Chicago, and he said to me, 'You should be the Dodgers' manager.' I said, 'One day, God willing.' And he said, 'When you do become manager, I'll come sing the National Anthem at your first game.'"

Sure enough, Sinatra sang at Dodger Stadium on April 7, 1977, Lasorda's first game that season as Dodgers manager.

This led to a problem for Sinatra in the 1977 World Series. The Dodgers were playing the New York Yankees. How did the man who sang "New York, New York" yet had befriended the Dodgers manager decide who to root for?

Before Game 6 at Yankee Stadium, Sinatra went to a restaurant near Yankee Stadium and was told that the Yankees were eating at the same restaurant. "Good," Sinatra said. "Tell them the Dodgers are coming."

So Sinatra threw his support to his friend, but he was smart enough not to close the door to the Yankees entirely. Before he left, he paid the Yankees' bill.

30–30–30–30

One of the first things Tommy Lasorda did when he took over as manager before the 1977 season started was to talk to his players

Dodgers fan Frank Sinatra keeps his promise to Tommy Lasorda and opens the team's 1977 season by singing the National Anthem in Los Angeles on April 7, 1977. *(AP Photo)*

individually and tell them what he expected. Most of it was rather routine, but he had special messages for two players: Steve Garvey and Dusty Baker.

Garvey was coming off of a season where he hit .317 with 13 homers, but Lasorda wanted something more from him—more homers. He told Garvey to start going for the long ball, even if it meant sacrificing some points off his batting average. Lasorda's theory was that the Dodgers would never be able to catch the Reds, who had won the last two World Series, unless they added more power to the lineup.

Lasorda's real project during that off-season was to rebuild the confidence of Dusty Baker. The Dodgers acquired Baker before the 1976 season for Jim Wynn, and Baker responded with the worst season of his career, hitting .242 with just four homers.

Lasorda talked to Baker and told him that no matter what, he would be in the starting lineup everyday and that Lasorda needed him if the Dodgers were going to win the title.

"No one ever told me that before," Baker said.

What Tommy Lasorda wants, Tommy Lasorda gets. The Dodgers became a power-hitting club, got off to a 22–4 start, and never looked back, winning the NL West by 10 games with a 98–64 record.

Garvey responded with 33 home runs in 1977 to go with a .297 average. Reggie Smith hit 32 homers, and Ron Cey contributed 30. Going into the last week of the season, a resurgent Baker had 29 home runs. No team in baseball history, not even the Murderer's Row 1927 Yankees, had four players with 30 or more home runs before.

Baker was still stuck on 29 going into the final game of the season, a Sunday afternoon game against the Houston Astros at Dodger Stadium. It didn't matter if they won or lost, so Lasorda gave most of his regulars the day off, except for Baker. J.R. Richard, one of the toughest pitchers in the game and a notorious Dodger killer, was on the mound for the Astros.

The fans that day knew the situation and treated every Baker at-bat as a special event. In the first inning, Baker singled to left, one of the few times you will ever see a home crowd disappointed by a base hit. In the fourth inning, pressing a little to get the shot he needed, Baker struck out. That brings us to the sixth inning.

Manny Mota led off the inning with a homer, so the crowd of 46,501 was already excited when Baker came to the plate. On a 1–2 count, Baker lifted a fastball over the left-field fence for home run No. 30.

Baker talked about the importance of the homer after the game.

"I'm sure that it has to provide us with an emotional boost going into the playoffs.

"I thank the Lord for all the wonderful things that have happened to me this year. This is my biggest moment yet. I have the same feeling today that I had on the night that Henry Aaron hit his 715th home run and I felt like I was the one who hit it."

Baker and Aaron were teammates on the Atlanta Braves when Aaron broke Babe Ruth's home-run record.

The long wait for home run No. 30 took its toll on Baker.

"I was really only swinging for home runs in the Friday and Saturday games, and the result was that I had several pop-ups that I normally wouldn't have. I went back to thinking in terms of line drives today for three reasons. One was that I want to be sharp for the playoffs. Two was that I had become a little tired from the pressure. The other was that with a line-drive stroke, I can still hit the ball out anywhere and I usually get my base hits, too."

The home run coming when it did was a bit of a surprise, if only because the Astros' Richard owned the Dodgers in his career. When his playing days ended in 1980 because of a stroke, Richard was 15–4 with a 1.86 ERA in 28 career appearances (24 starts) against the Dodgers.

Baker reflected on the homer in a 2011 interview.

"I certainly didn't think I'd hit No. 30 that day, not with Richard on the mound. I also knew my chances were dwindling and the odds were increasing against my getting the homer. The main thing I had on my mind wasn't hitting the homer but finishing with a .290 average. I just wanted to hit it hard. I didn't realize it was gone until I saw the outfielders give up on it."

And how did getting the record make him feel?

"I felt good for myself, for the team, for all the people pulling for me. If I hadn't hit it, I'd have walked around all winter unhappy, wondering why I couldn't have hit just one more. I'd have also been somewhat down going into the playoffs."

Steak Dinners for Everyone!

Baker's homer wasn't the only interesting part of the game. The home run that Manny Mota hit leading off the sixth inning was the first one he had hit in five seasons.

Mota had transitioned from full-time player to full-time pinch-hitter in 1974, so he got a limited number of at-bats each season and hadn't hit one out since 1972. When manager Tommy Lasorda sent Mota to the plate in the sixth inning, Dodgers pitcher Tommy John told him, "The next time out, why don't you see how far you can hit one."

Mota took the advice.

"I said to myself, *Okay, take one pitch and see if you can pull it. See if you can hit it. Okay, take one pitch and see if you can pull it, see if you can hit it hard.* It was a great feeling to run clear around the bases for the first time in five years."

So how does a steak dinner figure into all of this?

When Lasorda told Mota to grab a bat and pinch-hit, he turned to Davey Lopes—knowing what John had said to Mota—and said, "Wouldn't it be great if Manny hit a homer?"

Lopes, not knowing of the John-Mota conversation, rolled his eyes and said, "If he hits a home run, I'll buy everyone on the team a steak dinner."

After Mota homered, Lopes greeted Mota in the dugout by pretending to faint.

Reggie Hits Three

Okay, I guess we have to talk about it. It is a major moment in Dodgers history, and it would be great if the dugout walls could talk to us about it, so let's discuss it and get it out of the way—Reggie Jackson's three home runs in Game 6 of the 1977 World Series.

Tommy Lasorda made a stellar debut as Dodgers manager, guiding the team to its first World Series since 1974, but then he ran into the Yankees and their star right fielder, Reggie Jackson.

Jackson had a relatively quiet first three games, going 2-for-8. He got going in Game 4, homering in a 4–2 Yankees victory, and again in Game 5 during a 10–4 Dodgers victory.

Game 6 was in Yankee Stadium, and New York only needed one more victory to win the Series. The Dodgers sent Burt Hooton to the mound. He quickly got two runs to work with when Steve Garvey tripled home Reggie Smith and Ron Cey in the top of the first.

Jackson came to the plate for the first time in the second inning and walked on four pitches. He scored on Chris Chambliss' home run, tying the game 2–2. The Dodgers added a run in the third on Smith's homer. Then Jackson went to work. In the fourth inning with Thurman Munson on first, Jackson lined Hooton's first pitch to deep right for a homer.

Jackson broke down each homer on the one-year anniversary after the game for *Sports Illustrated.* "Well, the first homer put us ahead 4–3, so that was real enough. It was a hook shot into the stands."

The Yankees added another run in the fourth to make it 5–3 Yankees when Jackson came up again in the fifth inning. This time he was facing a new pitcher, Elias Sosa. On the first pitch Jackson hit a home run to deep right, scoring Willie Randolph.

"Before the second one," Jackson said, "I talked to [Yankees coach] Gene Michael and asked him what Elias Sosa threw. I knew I was going to hit the ball on the button after hearing from Gene, but I didn't know how quick it would come. That one iced the game 7–3."

The score remained 7–3 until the bottom of the eighth when Jackson came up again. Another new face was on the mound, knuckle-baller Charlie Hough. With the crowd on its feet and chanting, "Reg-gie! Reg-gie! Reg-gie!" Jackson's eyes grew wide as Hough floated a knuckler up to the plate. That first pitch resulted in a home run to deep center that was the icing on the cake of an 8–4 Yankees victory that gave them the World Series title.

"Before the last one, I saw Charlie Hough warming up," Jackson said. "A knuckleballer. Frank Robinson taught me how to hit that pitch in 1970 when he managed me in winter ball. I thought if I got a decent pitch I could hit another one out. Anyway, at that point I couldn't lose. All I had to do was show up at the plate. They were going to cheer me even if I struck out. So the last one was strictly dreamland. Nothing was going through my mind. Here it's a World Series game, it's going all over the country on TV, and all I'm thinking is, 'Hey man, wow, that's three.'"

The last home run was hit so far (some estimated it at 490 feet) that all Hough could do was joke about it after the game.

"I thought the wind blew mine out," Hough said. "No, he hit a good pitch. Down and away. Of course, he hits them down and away. Whatever it was, he exploded."

Lasorda was asked if he would have done anything differently if he had the chance to do it over again, and he responded with a classic line.

"I should have done one thing different. I should have never got out of bed this morning."

If you count the homer he hit in Game 5, Jackson hit home runs on his last four swings of the bat. An amazing accomplishment, even if it had to be a Yankee who did it.

"I must admit," said Steve Garvey after the game, "when Reggie Jackson hit his third home run and I was sure nobody was watching, I applauded into my glove."

Russell Wins It

October 7, 1977, is known as Black Friday in the city of Philadelphia, and whatever you do, don't mention Bill Russell's name to Phillies fans (not the Celtics center, the Dodgers shortstop).

After splitting the first two games of the NLCS at Dodger Stadium, the Phillies took a 5–3 lead into the ninth inning of Game 3. A series of misplays by Philadelphia resulted in a three-run rally and a 6–5 Dodgers win with Russell driving in the winning run. Los Angeles wrapped up the 1977 pennant the following night.

The Phillies and the Dodgers staged a rematch in the next year's NLCS. The Dodgers captured the first two games at Philadelphia, 9–5 and 4–0, before the Phillies stayed alive with a 9–4 victory behind Steve Carlton in Game 3 at Dodger Stadium.

Greg Luzinski hit a two-run homer in the top of the third to give the Phillies a 2–1 lead in Game 4. The Dodgers came back on homers by Ron Cey and Steve Garvey to take a 3–2 lead, but Bake McBride tied it again with a solo shot in the seventh.

It remained that way until the 10th inning. Phillies closer Tug McGraw got two quick outs, then walked Ron Cey, bringing Dusty Baker to the plate. Baker hit a soft liner to center fielder Garry Maddox, a multiple Gold Glove winner about whom Phillies announcer Harry

Kalas once said, "Two-thirds of the earth is covered by water, the other third is covered by Garry Maddox."

The ball hit Maddox right in the glove. Then it bounced out. A stunned Maddox picked it up and threw it back in. The improbable error put runners at first and second. There were two outs in the bottom of the 10th, and Bill Russell came to the plate.

"I was in the trainer's room, and we were listening on the radio," Rick Rhoden said when asked about the game. "When Russell came up, I told Bill Buhler [then the Dodgers' trainer], 'The game's over. Bill Russell is going to get a hit.' I just felt that there was no way we were going to lose that game with him up there."

Russell slashed a single to center. Again Maddox couldn't come up with the ball and Cey scored, giving the Dodgers the game and the NL pennant.

"I don't know why, but for some reason I went up there knowing I was going to get a hit," Russell said after the game. "There was no way I was going to strike out. I was getting tired, we had gone through a lot. It had been a long day and a long season, and I just wanted to end it. A lot of times you go up to the plate and you're nervous or not comfortable, but this time I wasn't nervous and I felt good. I was just hoping there was no play at the plate."

Russell was always considered one of the Dodgers' best clutch hitters, even though he was never known for his bat.

"Bill Russell carries a Ouija board around in his back pocket," Rick Monday recounted. "He could find a hole in any defense, and he found the sweetest possible hole that time."

The Death of Jim Gilliam

Want to win a bet? Ask a Dodgers fan to name the player who has appeared in the most World Series with the team. Give them three guesses. Heck, give them five. They probably won't guess the answer.

Jim Gilliam played in seven World Series for the Dodgers and was the glue that held many of those teams together. He made his debut with the team in 1953, when the Dodgers were still in Brooklyn (Gilliam was named Rookie of the Year), and he retired after the 1966 season.

If you needed a position filled, Gilliam was your man. Need him to play second base for the season? Done. Third base? No problem. Injured outfielder and you need a replacement for a few games? Gilliam is your man.

Gilliam came west with the team in 1958 and led the NL in walks in 1959 when the Dodgers won the World Series. He started at third base from 1958 to 1960 and then at second from 1961 to 1963.

He was named a coach after the 1964 season and planned to retire as a player, but injuries put him back on the field and he was the starting third baseman for the 1965 World Series champs and the 1966 NL pennant winners. In his career, he made two All-Star teams and finished in the top 10 in NL MVP voting twice. His relatively low .265 batting average is offset by his .360 on-base percentage.

Gilliam finally retired after the 1966 season and became a full-time coach for the team. He was only 38 years old and thus one of the youngest coaches in the game.

One thing about "Junior," as his friends called him—he commanded respect. He worked with young players to make them better and always had a tip or two for veterans. He was the Dodgers' first-base coach in 1978, helping guide the team into the playoffs. On September 15, two weeks before the end of the season, Gilliam suffered a cerebral hemorrhage and was in a coma.

The Dodgers won the NLCS over the Phillies that year, but before they could celebrate, tragedy struck—Gilliam, still hospitalized and in a coma, died of a massive heart attack the day after the Dodgers won the pennant.

Team captain Davey Lopes, who was probably closer to Gilliam than anyone else on the team, spoke about their fallen comrade. "It's hard to express what he meant to us. He was respected and loved by all of us. It's going to be very difficult not to keep thinking about him. Everything

Jim Gilliam crosses the plate, giving the Dodgers a 2–1 win—and the World Series title—against the Yankees in Los Angeles on October 6, 1963. Catcher Elston Howard of the Yanks is at right. *(AP Photo)*

associated with baseball will automatically make us think of Jim Gilliam. They say time heals all wounds, but it's going to take a long, long time."

Tommy Lasorda, who was named manager over Gilliam before the 1977 season, remembered his longtime friend. "Jim and I were friends for 28 years. He's one of the very, very few guys I've ever seen in baseball that nobody had anything bad to say about. I remember when he broke in. A lot of black players in the big leagues were having problems, and he had to go through troubled days. But I never heard him utter a word of resentment. He was loved by everyone on this club and in this organization. Nobody connected with the game has ever done more for his race. The Lord took a truly great man from us."

Thirty-five years after Gilliam's death, Vin Scully shared his thoughts. "I once introduced Jim Gilliam. Well, I was introducing the team, and I would introduce, 'So and so is the shortstop' and so on, and I introduced Jim as 'Jim Gilliam, baseball player.'

"He was one of the smartest players. I remember Walter Alston saying that Jim never missed a sign. Never. Like anyone else, you are going to drop a ball, you are going to make an error, but Jim never made a mental mistake. And on the basepaths, he'd go from first to third all the time. He always did the right thing.

"He was very quiet and not at all 'on,' but he was a consummate baseball player.

"He was married in St. Louis, and the team bus stopped at the reception while the photographer was taking pictures. Jim said to the photographer, 'One more.' The photographer took it, and Jim got on the bus and we went to Busch Stadium.

"He was the ultimate. Quiet, just great."

The Dodgers retired Gilliam's No. 19 shortly after he died. He remains the only Dodger whose number has been retired who is not in the Hall of Fame.

It's a well-deserved honor for a quiet legend.

One last thing. One of my favorite baseball books of all time is *The Bronx Zoo* by Sparky Lyle and Peter Golenbock. The book recounts the 1978 season of the New York Yankees through the eyes of Lyle, one of their top relievers.

In it, Lyle criticizes Lopes, saying, "In those first couple of games in L.A., the only games they win, Lopes was hitting home runs and circling the bases with his finger pointing in the air, as if to say, 'We're number one.' How bush is that?"

But Lyle is wrong. Lopes was pointing to heaven, acknowledging Gilliam.

I just wanted to set the record straight.

Welch Strikes Out Reggie

The 1978 World Series was a rematch between the Dodgers and Yankees. After Reggie Jackson's amazing three-homer performance in the deciding game of the 1977 World Series, Dodgers fans were alternately looking forward to getting a chance to beat him and dreading having to face him again.

Game 1 was the best and worst of both worlds. The Dodgers won in a rout 11–5, but Jackson homered.

Game 2 was more of a nail-biter. It was the last game at Dodger Stadium before the Series moved to New York for Games 3, 4, and 5. Heading east with a 2–0 Series lead would be a lot better than heading back tied 1–1. So, of course, the game came down to the final out with Jackson at the plate.

The Yankees had scored two runs off Burt Hooton in the top of the third when Jackson doubled to right, scoring Roy White and Thurman Munson. The Dodgers scored a run in the fourth on Ron Cey's single (scoring Reggie Smith) and three more in the sixth when Cey homered to left off future Hall of Famer Catfish Hunter.

Cey said Smith predicted his homer before he hit it. "He told me that as soon as Hunter got out of a jam [Hunter got Steve Garvey to pop out in the at-bat before Cey's homer], he just knew Catfish would make a mistake. He told me he just knew.

"It's one of those things that happens maybe once or twice in a season. It's just a feeling, an impulse, an instinct. It's hard to explain unless you've played the game."

The home run brought the Dodger Stadium crowd to life, and the fans rarely sat down for the remainder of the game.

"It's extremely difficult to block out the emotions of the fans," Cey said. "Of course I feel it. It's just beautiful."

Jackson drove in another run for the Yankees in the seventh inning, making the score 4–3 Dodgers. It remained that way until the top of the ninth.

Terry Forster, the Dodgers' closer who had 22 saves during the season, was on the mound.

Bucky Dent led off with a single and moved to second on Roy White's grounder back to the mound. Forster then lost command, walking Paul Blair on five pitches. That brought manager Tommy Lasorda to the mound.

Lasorda had a decision to make. Thurman Munson and Jackson were up next for the Yankees. Forster was obviously tiring, and warming up in the bullpen was Bob Welch, who threw a 95-mph fastball and had been superb the last two months of the season. But Welch was a rookie, untested in high-pressure situations, and would have to retire the Yankees' two best clutch hitters.

Lasorda decided to go with Welch.

As Welch walked to the mound, the entire infield, Garvey, Lopes, Russell, Cey, and Steve Yeager, gathered at the mound. When Welch got to the mound, Lopes, the Dodgers' team captain, had a few motivational words for him.

"I told him to go after them as hard as you can. Throw like you've never thrown in your life. Nothing fazes that man. He's got tremendous poise, he's got ungodly talent."

Welch threw a strike to Munson before retiring him on a fly ball to right.

That set the stage. Welch vs. Jackson. Rookie vs. veteran. Power pitcher vs. power hitter.

"I've been in some tough situations before, coming out of the bullpen," Welch said. "I knew I was going to have to face Munson first. Tommy just gave me the ball and said to throw strikes. I just wanted to go after them and make them hit my pitch."

Yeager, the catcher, had one plan in mind—nothing but fastballs.

"I didn't have any other pitch in mind," Yeager said. "I knew if we threw him a changeup, Reggie would probably screw himself into the ground, but if I'm gonna get the kid hurt, I'm gonna do it with his fastball."

First pitch: Fastball up and in. Reggie swings and misses, swinging so hard that he falls to one knee. Strike one.

Second pitch: Fastball up high and inside, sending Jackson sprawling to the turf. Ball one.

Lopes remembers what it was like watching this duel. "I knew the ball wasn't going to be hit to me, so I just stood there and watched like a spectator. I knew Reggie would either strike out or hit it nine miles."

Third pitch: Fastball away. Jackson fouls it off to the third-base seats. Strike two.

Fourth pitch: Fastball inside. Jackson fouls it straight back.

Fifth pitch: Fastball high. Jackson fouls it back.

Sixth pitch: Fastball high. Ball two. Count is two balls, two strikes.

At this point, with Welch ready to pitch, Jackson calls time and steps out of the batter's box.

"There was a psychological game going on," Lopes said. "Reggie was trying to make the kid wait, but it didn't bother him."

Seventh pitch: Fastball inside. Jackson fouls it back.

Eighth pitch: Fastball high. Full count.

Ninth pitch: Fastball inside. Jackson swings and misses. The crowd explodes in jubilation as the Dodgers race and swarm their rookie pitcher.

"That last pitch was unbelievable," Yeager said. "I don't know if they had a clock on it, but it was moving, it got to me in a hurry."

How close did Jackson come to connecting?

"He just missed it," Welch said after the game. "He missed it just enough. The first pitch I threw him was the one he really had a chance to hit, that was the one."

Jackson was irate after striking out, storming back to the Yankees dugout and slamming his bat against the wall. The bat accidentally grazed Yankees manager Bob Lemon.

"I was emotional, and it's unlike me to be that way in a game," Jackson said.

Lemon had no problem with Jackson's anger.

"The guy was hyped up," Lemon said. "He'd just struck out to end a World Series game. I didn't expect him to walk into the dugout and set his bat and helmet down gently and say, 'Gee fellas, I'm sorry I struck out.' He was hot, and we should have got out of his way."

But all focus after the game remained where it should have been— on Welch. His teammates were effusive in their praise.

"It was unbelievable," Yeager said.

"That boy can pitch," center fielder Bill North said. "I looked at people in the stands, looked all around the ballpark and said, 'This is what the World Series is all about.'"

"He's just an ordinary 21-year-old who has a 150-mile-an-hour fastball," Rick Monday said.

Hip, Hip, Boo

Dodgers fans have replayed it dozens of times in their head. Game 4 of the 1978 World Series, and the Dodgers were up 2–1 in the Series and had a 3–0 lead in the sixth inning when Reggie Jackson, yes, him again, stuck his hip into things.

With runners on first and second and one out, Jackson singled to right, scoring Roy White and moving Thurman Munson to second. The next batter, Lou Piniella, hit a soft liner to shortstop that Bill Russell looked like he could catch but instead let it bounce first. It looked like an easy double play. Russell stepped on second to force Jackson then threw to first. Jackson, standing between first and second, thrust out his right hip and the ball hit him, caroming down the right-field line. As first baseman Steve Garvey argued for an interference call from first-base umpire Frank Pulli, Munson scored.

An irate Tommy Lasorda argued till his face almost turned blue, but the umpires refused to call interference. The run counted, making it 3–2. The Yankees tied it in the eighth and won it in the bottom of the 10th, evening the Series at 2–2. They would go on to win it all in six games. If not for Reggie Jackson's hip, the Yankees never would have tied Game 4, and the Dodgers would have won to go up 3–1 in the Series, virtually assuring them a World Series title.

At least, that's the story Dodgers fans believe—and we're sticking to it.

In the aftermath of the game, the Dodgers knew they were robbed of a victory.

"That's illegal," Garvey said. "The ump said Reggie didn't have to get out of the way, but the guy can't move into it, can he? It was a great play on Reggie's part. He got away with it, and you've got to give him credit.

"It was intentional interference, but the umpire didn't feel it was interference. Reggie was facing square to second base, and as the ball came he just kind of shifted his weight, shifted toward the ball. It was a very tough way to lose. It was quick thinking on his part, but it was also dirty pool."

Perhaps the most angry Dodger was second baseman Davey Lopes. "You saw it, why ask me?" he said to reporters after the game. "I'm not going to tell you anything different than what you saw, so don't even ask."

Of course, lost in all the furor was the fact the Yankees were still trailing 3–2 after the play. It was still the Dodgers' game to win.

But the loss still hurts after all these years. Lasorda and Jackson were guests of Joe Buck during a game televised on the FOX network in 2010. Lasorda's first comment to Jackson, "Reggie, will you finally admit you stuck your hip into that ball?"

In 2013, third baseman Ron Cey was asked about the play. "The interference issue with Reggie Jackson was the one that pulled the rug right out from under us, and that's still my biggest nightmare in base-ball," Cey told MLB.com. "If the call is made properly and if they huddled together like they should have, we would have walked off the field with a 3–0 lead. We end up losing that game. The next day we were flat, deflated. And so I feel legitimately that '78 was the one that got away, and it's still hard to talk about."

Mota Breaks the Record

When I was a kid and would watch the Dodgers play, two of my favorite players were Vic Davalillo and Manny Mota. To my adolescent eyes, they each seemed to be about 60 years old (they both were actually around 40), and all they would do is pinch-hit, seemingly coming up with game-winning hit after game-winning hit. Especially Mota, who was a wizard with the bat.

In a role you just never see anymore, Mota was only a pinch-hitter for his last seven seasons with the Dodgers. His at-bat totals, starting in

1974, were 57, 49, 52, 38, 33, and 42. And that's in full seasons with the team.

So it was really no surprise that as the 1979 season was coming to a close, Mota was closing in on the all-time pinch-hit record held by Smoky Burgess, who had 144 career pinch hits between 1949 and 1967.

Mota approached pinch-hitting as a science, preparing himself early in the game for the possibility he would be called upon in the seventh, eighth, or ninth inning.

"The first thing about pinch-hitting is you have to like it," Mota said, reflecting on his great pinch-hitting career. "Most players can't accept that role. Second, you have to work harder, to keep your edge physically and mentally. You have to know the strike zone. You have to relax, be patient. You can't try to hit the ball too hard, just meet it."

Mota came into the game on September 2, 1979, tied with Burgess, but he had been tied with him for almost a month. Mota's last pinch-hit had come on August 6, and he had been 0-for-6 as a pinch-hitter since that date.

Lynn McGlothen was pitching for the Cubs when Mota was called upon to bat for pitcher Ken Brett. Mota took two quick strikes and a ball then laced a single to right, giving him the record.

"To be honest, I was thinking of the record," Mota said after the game. "After the seventh inning, I thought I would pinch-hit and I went back into the clubhouse to take a few swings. All I could think of was the record."

Mota's teammates were just as happy as he was.

"He's a great hitter and a great person," Davey Lopes said. "He's the most respected player on the team."

Here's a little-known fact—Mota's wife, Marguerite, was taking care of their eight kids and was very late getting to the game (as anyone with eight kids would be). She heard the pinch-hit on the car radio, pulled to the side of the parking lot, and gave each one of her kids a hug while crying, proud of her husband.

"People thought they had gone crazy," Mota said.

Mota became a Dodgers coach after the season, a role he held until 2013.

CHAPTER 4
THE 1980s

Reuss Rolls to a No-Hitter

Ask Jerry Reuss what he remembers most about his no-hitter against the Dodgers, and you might think he would mention the final out or maybe the relief and exultation after that final out. But he might just mention one other thing—dropping a batting helmet on Tommy Lasorda's head.

The date was June 27, 1980. The scene was Candlestick Park, home of the Dodgers' arch-nemesis San Francisco Giants. The Dodgers hadn't had a no-hitter since Bill Singer threw one in 1970.

Reuss took the mound and had a feeling something special would happen. "I was aware of a no-hitter from the very first pitch," Reuss said in 2013. "After three hitless innings, I sensed there was a possibility. After six innings and an eight-run lead, I started counting down the remaining outs. With each out, the reality was closer."

And what exactly happened with that helmet and Lasorda?

"The things I'm remembering now, the little things, are starting to come to me," Reuss said. "Like when I knocked the helmet down on Lasorda. I was reaching for my glove. I just had to laugh."

Lasorda remembers it, too.

"It just came right flat down on my head," Lasorda said. "At first I was mad, then I said, 'Jerry, just go out there and do what you were doing. Don't do anything different.'"

The no-hitter could have been a perfect game, except shortstop Bill Russell fielded a grounder by Jack Clark in the first inning and threw the ball away for an error. Clark was the only Giants batter to reach base during the game, the error costing Reuss a chance at a perfect game. But Reuss, who was quite the prankster while he was a Dodger, did not give Russell a hard time.

"Russell made numerous fielding plays in the game and also went 3-for-5 at bat," Reuss pointed out.

"I screwed up," Russell said good-naturedly after the game. "But the least Reuss can do is walk a guy and take me off the hook."

The best defensive play came in the eighth inning when third baseman Ron Cey made a diving stop of a Larry Herndon smash and threw to first in time to retire him.

Reuss said he wasn't worried throughout the game. "What was there to worry about? Nothing happens until I do something."

Sweeping the Astros

The Dodgers turned it around after the disappointing 1979 season and remained in contention for the NL West throughout the season.

At the end of play on October 2, the Astros led the Dodgers by three games, with three games left to play for each team. And those three games would be against each other at Dodger Stadium. The Dodgers needed to sweep all three games to force a one-game playoff.

Here's what happened.

Game 1, October 3: Ken Forsch started for the Astros against Don Sutton. It was a classic pitcher's duel. The Astros scored a run in the top of the second when Forsch singled to score Alan Ashby. The Dodgers tied it in the fourth when Steve Garvey singled home Rick Monday only to fall behind 2–1 when Cesar Cedeno scored on Ashby's sacrifice fly in the top of the eighth.

So it was 2–1 going into the bottom of the ninth, and the Dodgers were three outs away from being eliminated from playoff contention. Jay Johnstone grounded to second. Monday singled to right and was replaced by Rudy Law, a much faster runner, at first base. Dusty Baker hit a grounder to second, but Rafael Landestoy couldn't handle it and was charged with an error, putting runners at first and second with one out. With the crowd rocking Dodger Stadium, Garvey flied out to center, bringing Ron Cey to the plate. He singled to center to score the tying run, and the game went to extra innings when Pedro Guerrero grounded to short.

The Astros were retired in order in the top of the 10th by a rookie left-hander named Fernando Valenzuela. That brought the dramatic bottom of the 10th. Joe Ferguson led off for the Dodgers against Forsch, still in the game for the Astros.

Ferguson hit one of the most dramatic homers in team history, belting a Forsch fastball over the fence to give the Dodgers a 3–2 win and send the crowd into a frenzy never heard before in Dodger Stadium history. I was at that game, and the screaming was so loud, all you could hear was a high-pitched whine. It was like you were at a Justin Bieber concert years before he was even born.

"I've never heard anything like it, ever," Ferguson said after the game. But the Dodgers still needed to win the next two to make the homer truly special.

Game 2, October 4: Jerry Reuss pitched fearlessly, capping a season during which he threw a no-hitter vs. Nolan Ryan, who was at the height of his powers. It was also the least dramatic of the three games. The Dodgers scored in the second inning when Derrel Thomas singled to left with runners on first and second and two out, scoring Garvey. The Astros tied it in the top of the fourth when Art Howe singled in Jose Cruz. The Dodgers retook the lead in the bottom of the inning when Garvey led off with a home run.

And that's the way it ended. Reuss pitched a masterful game, giving up seven hits and striking out seven while increasing his record to 18–6.

Game 3, October 5: This was it. Either win and tie the Astros or lose and go home.

The Astros jumped out to a 2–0 lead in the top of the second when consecutive singles by Ashby and Craig Reynolds scored Cedeno and Howe. Showing just how important this game was, Lasorda had a quick hook, pulling Hooton after Reynolds' single. Bobby Castillo settled things down, getting out of the inning with no further damage. Ruhle, who was bothered by blisters on his pitching hand, came out in the third inning and was replaced by Joaquin Andujar.

The Astros tacked on another run in the fourth when Terry Puhl doubled home Ashby. It was 3–0 Astros after four innings.

In the bottom of the fifth, Ferguson grounded to short, but singles by Thomas, Gary Thomasson, and Davey Lopes scored a run and forced Astros manager Bill Virdon to go to his bullpen again, bringing in Joe Sambito who got Mickey Hatcher to ground into an inning-ending double play.

The game stayed 3–1 until the bottom of the seventh when Pedro Guerrero led off with a single and moved to second on Ferguson's base hit. Derrel Thomas laid down a perfect sacrifice, putting runners on second and third with one out.

It was then that Tommy Lasorda reached into his bag of tricks and pulled out Manny Mota, who was the Dodgers' first-base coach. Mota, considered by many the greatest pinch-hitter in baseball history, had been placed on the active roster when rosters expanded in September.

So Dodgers fans were treated to the sight of the first-base coach walking into the dugout, grabbing a bat, and hitting for the pitcher.

This story wouldn't be any fun if Mota struck out, and he didn't. He singled to right, scoring Guerrero and taking second on the throw home. Unfortunately, that's exactly how the inning ended. The score after seven was Astros 3, Dodgers 2.

Frank Lacorte was pitching for the Astros in the bottom of the eighth when Ron Cey stepped to the plate with Steve Garvey, who had reached on an error by Enos Cabell, on first.

Cey was playing on a sprained ankle. If this game had been played in June, he wouldn't have been in the lineup. Heck, if it were June, he's probably have been on the 15-day disabled list.

On a full-count pitch, Cey homered. The Dodgers led 4–3.

"I was looking for a pitch to drive," Cey said after the game. "I wasn't thinking about the pain. I wasn't thinking home run, but I thought that on a 3–2 pitch, I might get one I could handle."

There was still the top of the ninth to play, and the Dodgers had a rookie, Steve Howe, on the mound. Tommy Lasorda was notorious for not trusting rookies in key situations, and he had a plan. Don Sutton took over as first-base coach when Mota pinch-hit, so Sutton was sitting in the dugout. The Dodgers' manager walked by him and asked him if he could pitch. Moments later, Sutton was in the bullpen, warming up.

Meanwhile, Howe retired Jeffrey Leonard on a foul ball to right. Gary Woods singled, and Terry Puhl forced him at second. One out away, and man on first for the Astros. Enos Cabell, whose error opened the door for the Dodgers in the eighth, was at the plate. He hit a single to left, and the Astros had runners on first and third.

Lasorda went out to the mound, and Sutton came in the game.

It took Sutton two pitches to retire Denny Walling on a grounder to second. It took 30 minutes for the fans to stop cheering. It was a love affair all weekend between the Dodgers and the fans.

"It would be easier to cap a nuclear reactor than the excitement we have had here," Sutton said. "For the first time in my 15 years here, it feels like we have a 10th man in the stands. It's very exciting to be a part of."

It was the last pitch Sutton would throw in a Dodgers uniform for eight years. He left the team as a free agent after the season to sign with—the Houston Astros.

As for the one-game playoff to decide the division title? The less said about that the better. The Dodgers lost 7–1. And whatever you do, don't say the name "Dave Goltz" to a Dodgers fan.

Fernandomania

After nearly winning the NL West in 1980, many experts pegged the Dodgers as the team to beat heading into the 1981 exhibition season. The team had a great pitching staff led by Jerry Reuss, Burt Hooton, and Bob Welch. Dave Goltz couldn't possibly be as bad as he was in 1980. And they could probably find another starter somewhere.

When injuries sidelined Reuss and Hooton, preventing them from starting on opening day, manager Tommy Lasorda rolled the dice and turned to that No. 5 starter, a guy who happened to be their best pitcher in spring training, Fernando Valenzuela.

Fernando (calling him Valenzuela just seems wrong for some reason), was only 20 years old, spoke little English, and was thrust onto the mound on opening day to pitch against the defending NL West champion Houston Astros.

All he did was shut them out and take his first step toward immortality, as far as Dodgers fans were concerned.

Fans turned out in droves to Dodgers games when Fernando pitched. Eleven of his 12 starts at Dodger Stadium in 1981 were sellouts. The team's attendance went up by an average of 7,519 fans at his home starts and an amazing 14,292 for road starts.

"I truly believe that there is no other player in major league history who created more new fans than Fernando Valenzuela," longtime Dodgers Spanish broadcaster Jamie Jarrin said in a 2006 *Dodger Magazine* interview. "Sandy Koufax, Don Drysdale, Joe DiMaggio, even Babe Ruth did not. Fernando turned so many people from Mexico, Central America, South America, into fans. He created interest in baseball among people who did not care about baseball."

Vin Scully was equally impressed. "I truly feel that Fernando was a religious experience for many people. You'd see parents with the little youngsters by the hand, using him as inspiration."

Los Angeles Dodgers owner Peter O'Malley (left) and manager Tommy Lasorda (right) with newly named National League Cy Young Award winner Fernando Valenzuela in Los Angeles on Wednesday, November 11, 1981. Valenzuela was the first rookie to receive the award. *(AP Photo/McLendon)*

But it had to be a fluke, right? There's no way that he could do that in his next start. Yeah, he could. Fernando went 8–0 in his first eight starts with seven complete games, five shutouts, and a 0.50 ERA. The stuff of legend. And baseball fans everywhere noticed as "Fernandomania" was born.

Some people didn't believe Fernando was really 20, and he got so many questions about it that Dodgers GM Al Campanis kept a copy of Fernando's birth certificate in his desk.

Some people thought Fernando had to be older—no rookie could pitch that well, have that much command. He even had an answer for them, a sentence he learned quickly in English and used often after games, "When I get on the mound, I don't know what afraid is."

Fernando finished the season 13–7 with a 2.48 ERA and became the first pitcher to win the Rookie of the Year Award and Cy Young Award in the same season. When he accepted the Cy Young Award, he was asked if he knew who Cy Young was.

"I do not know who he was, but a trophy carries his name so he must be someone very special to baseball."

So were you, Fernando. So were you.

Finally!

The Dodgers had not won a World Series since 1965, losing in 1966, 1974, 1977, and 1978. Not only that, the Garvey-Lopes-Russell-Cey infield was on its last legs. If they were going into the history books as champions, it had to be now.

Led by Fernando Valenzuela, the Dodgers got off to a strong start in 1981 and were in first place in the NL West, a half-game ahead of the Cincinnati Reds with a 36–21 record after the games on June 11 were played.

And then the players went out on strike, canceling the games between June 12 and August 9.

When a settlement to the strike was reached, there was much discussion about what to do with the season. Should they just pick up the season on August 10, play out the rest of the schedule, and whoever finishes in first wins each division? Should they make the team that wins each division after the games from August 10 to the end of the season play the team in each division with the best overall record in a mini-playoff?

Commissioner Bowie Kuhn considered it carefully and decided on the following. Whichever teams were in first place when the strike began would be declared first-half champion, and they would face the teams with the best record in the second half of the season in each division in a five-game divisional series to determine the division champions. (If

Outfielder Pedro Guerrero (left), catcher Steve Yeager (center), and third baseman Ron Cey (right) were named the Most Valuable Players in the World Series and celebrated after the Dodgers won in New York on Wednesday, October 28, 1981. *(AP Photo/STF)*

one team had won both halves, they would have faced the team with the next-best overall record.)

That decision has led to years and years of Cincinnati Reds fans complaining because, while the Reds had the best record in the NL West in 1981, they didn't win either the first or second half, leaving them on the outside looking in.

However, Reds fans overlook something very important, something Dodgers manager Tommy Lasorda did in the second half that hurt the team's overall record but set them up nicely for the playoffs and the future.

Knowing his team had a playoff berth sewn up no matter how they played in the second half, Lasorda gave a lot of playing time to younger players and his bench guys. Steve Sax, who would go on to win Rookie of the Year in 1982, got several starts at second base. Jay Johnstone, normally their top pinch-hitter, got more playing time to keep his bat sharp. Mike Scioscia got more time behind the plate to give aging veteran Steve Yeager some extra rest.

It was a brilliant plan by Lasorda, and it paid off beautifully in the playoffs.

The first-ever NL Division Series pitted the West's first-half champion, the Dodgers, against the second-half champion, the Houston Astros. Over in the NL East, the first-half champion Philadelphia Phillies took on the second-half champs, the Montreal Expos.

The series opened in the Astrodome, and the Astros jumped out to a 2–0 series lead, making it look like the Dodgers tenure in the playoffs would be short-lived. But the Dodgers stormed back to win the final three games of the series thanks to strong pitching by Burt Hooton, Valenzuela, and Jerry Reuss and key homers by Steve Garvey and Pedro Guerrero.

Up next, in the traditional best-of-five NL Championship Series, were the Montreal Expos, who had made the playoffs for the first time and had defeated the Phillies in the NL East division series 3–2.

Again, the Dodgers found themselves in a hole, winning Game 1 but losing Games 2 and 3. Game 4 was a rout, with Garvey homering and Dusty Baker driving in three runs in a 7–1 victory. That set up the pivotal Game 5 in Montreal.

Game 5 was a pitcher's duel between Valenzuela and Montreal's Ray Burris. The score was tied 1–1 in the bottom of the eighth when Expos manager Jim Fanning sent Tim Wallach to pinch-hit for Burris with one out and the bases empty.

"I wanted someone like Wallach who could hit the ball out," Fanning explained afterward.

Strange reasoning, since Wallach had hit only four homers that season and Burris seemed to have the Dodgers' number, shutting them out in Game 2 and holding them to a run and five hits in Game 5. Valenzuela retired Wallach on a grounder, and the score remained 1–1 when the inning ended.

Fanning had a decision to make going into the top of the ninth—who should be brought in to relieve Burris? He had left-hander Woodie Fryman, who had a 1.88 ERA and seven saves during the season, and right-hander Jeff Reardon, who had a 1.30 ERA and eight saves.

Who to choose?

Fanning went with Steve Rogers, the Expos' best starting pitcher, but he hadn't pitched in relief since 1978.

Rogers retired Garvey and Ron Cey to start the inning, bringing Rick Monday to the plate. Monday's eyes lit up when he saw the first pitch, a belt-high fastball, but he fouled it back.

"I said to myself, *You won't get another one like that*," Monday said. "But I got a better one."

With the count 3–1, Rogers grooved another fastball. This time Monday launched it over the center-field fence. But Monday lost track of the ball and didn't immediately realize he had homered.

"I didn't know where the heck the ball was," Monday said. "I had to look at the outfielders to see where the ball went. I saw the two outfielders turn at the wall, and then realized that it went out of the park. I almost fell down between second and third."

Pedro Guerrero struck out to end the inning, but there was still a bottom of the ninth to be played.

With Valenzuela still pitching, Rodney Scott led off with a grounder to first and Andre Dawson flied out to right to put the Dodgers one out away from the World Series. Valenzuela then lost his command, walking Gary Carter and Larry Parrish. With switch-hitter Jerry White due next, manager Tommy Lasorda went to the mound and removed his ace left-hander.

"First, I think Fernando was trying to be too careful. And second, we wanted to make White bat from the left side rather than from the right. He's better from the right."

Much like Fanning, Lasorda opted to bypass his closer, Steve Howe, for a starting pitcher, Bob Welch. It paid off for him, though, as Welch retired White on a grounder to second.

The Dodgers were headed to the World Series again to face their vaunted enemy, the New York Yankees.

Just to keep things consistent, the Dodgers fell into a 2–0 hole in the Series, losing Game 1 by a score of 5–3 and losing Game 2 in a 3–0 shutout. Both games were held at Yankee Stadium.

Games 3, 4, and 5 were played at Dodger Stadium, and that's when the Dodgers turned things around, thanks in part to those players to whom Lasorda gave some second-half playing time.

Valenzuela's performance in Game 3 can be best described with one word—gutty. He seemed to be in trouble every inning, but he somehow managed to pitch a complete game, giving up nine hits and walking seven in a 5–4 victory. The Yankees seemed to threaten to blow open the game every inning, and Valenzuela escaped every serious jam. In the eighth inning, Aurelio Rodriguez and Larry Milbourne singled to put runners on first and second with none out. Bobby Murcer came up to pinch-hit for pitcher Rudy May. Murcer was a power hitter who finished his career with 252 homers. In a surprise move, he tried to bunt and popped the ball foul between third base and the dugout. Ron Cey raced in and dove for the ball, catching it and then doubling Milbourne off of first to effectively end the Yankees' final threat of the game.

Afterward, Lasorda was asked why he stayed with Fernando for the whole game.

"I thought about taking him out, but I said to myself, *This is the year of Fernando*. That was one of the guttiest performances I've ever seen a young man do. He was like a championship poker player, bluffing his way through a hand."

Cey was also a star of the game, not only making that great defensive play, but hitting a three-run homer in the first inning.

The losing pitcher for the Yankees, by the way, was reliever George Frazier. That becomes important later.

Game 4 was a hitters' paradise, with runs being scored in every inning except the fourth and the ninth. Ten pitchers were used in the game, but the heroes for the Dodgers were Jay Johnstone and Steve Yeager.

It was 6–3 Yankees in the bottom of the sixth when Johnstone pinch-hit for Tom Niedenfuer. Johnstone slammed a two-run homer to bring the Dodgers to 6–5. The Dodgers scored two more in the bottom of the seventh with Yeager's sacrifice fly knocking in the go-ahead run, and they held on for an 8–7 victory.

The losing pitcher for the Yankees was George Frazier.

Game 5 matched two veteran left-handers as the Dodgers sent Jerry Reuss up against Ron Guidry.

The Yankees scored in the second inning when Lou Piniella singled to score Reggie Jackson. It stayed that way until the bottom of the seventh.

Guidry appeared to be cruising after he struck out Dusty Baker leading off the seventh, bringing Pedro Guerrero to the plate. On an 0–1 pitch, Guerrero launched a ball to deep left-center to tie the score. Four pitches later, Yeager launched a ball to almost the identical spot in left-center, giving the Dodgers a 2–1 lead.

The worst moment of the game for the Dodgers came in the eighth inning. Goose Gossage, a future Hall of Famer who owned a blazing fastball, let go of a 94-mph heater that hit Ron Cey square in the helmet. The thwack of the ball hitting the helmet reverberated around the stadium, the ball ricocheted down the third-base line, Cey collapsed to the ground, holding his head, and the fans grew deathly quiet.

And no one felt worse than Gossage. "I was saying to myself, *Oh, God*. If he doesn't have the helmet, he might be dead. I kept saying 'Get up, get up.' There was nothing more I could do.

"Sure you want to win the game at any expense. But not this one. There was no way I was throwing at him. I generally try to throw my fastball right down the middle, but with Cey I was trying to keep it up. The ball sailed. There was nothing I could do about it."

Gossage was one of the classiest major leaguers of all time, and to a man, not one Dodger believed he was throwing at Cey. It was just one of those things that happen in the game.

Cey walked off the field but was uninjured and returned to play in Game 6. Meanwhile, the Dodgers held on to their 2–1 lead and took a 3–2 Series lead.

Then, one of the strangest moments in World Series history happened, and it didn't take place anywhere near a stadium. Around midnight in Los Angeles, the phone started ringing in the various hotel rooms of media assigned to cover the World Series. There was going to be a news conference in the hotel lobby, and everyone needed to be there.

As the sleepy reporters entered a conference room, they saw Yankees owner George Steinbrenner standing there with a cast on his left hand and a cut lip.

Steinbrenner said he got into the hotel elevator some time after Game 5, where he was joined by two Dodgers fans. The Dodgers fans start mocking Steinbrenner and his team, and he responded by beating up both fans and tossing them out of the elevator.

"It's okay for me to criticize my players because I write the checks," Steinbrenner said. "One guy said the Yankees had 'animal fans,' and I guess that did it. I hit him, and he hit me in the side of the head with a bottle. I know he's missing three teeth. He's probably still looking for them. I hit him with a right, and he went down. I guess the other guy hit me, which probably accounts for my lip."

There were no witnesses to the fight, and the two men Steinbrenner beat up have never come forward to be identified, leaving some to wonder if he made up the whole thing to fire up his team. Steinbrenner, who died in 2010, went to his grave swearing the story was true.

The teams returned to New York for Game 6.

The key moment of the game came in the bottom of the fourth. With the score tied 1–1, the Yankees had two runners on with two out and their starting pitcher, Tommy John, due up. John had gone 9–8 with a 2.63 ERA in 1981 and had held the Dodgers to one run in 13 innings during the World Series. Plus, the Yankees bullpen had been unsteady during the Series.

Manager Bob Lemon decided to hit for John, sending Bobby Murcer to the plate. John was irate, and the TV cameras caught him saying, "Unbeliev-able!" in the Yankees dugout.

Murcer flied out to end the inning, making Lemon's decision look even worse.

"I wanted to get some runs," Lemon said. "I didn't think it was a gamble. I've seen John look better. He'd given up six hits in four innings. I just thought I'd make a move then, get some runs."

Lemon replaced John on the mound with George Frazier. Here's what happened. Single by Davey Lopes. Sacrifice by Bill Russell. Fly out by Steve Garvey. Single by Cey. Single by Baker. Triple by Guerrero. Monday strikes out. Three runs scored, and it was 4–1 Dodgers.

The wheels then came off for the Yankees. The Dodgers scored four more times in the sixth and once in the eighth to win Game 6 9–2 and take the World Series.

The losing pitcher was George Frazier, who became the first pitcher to lose three games in one World Series.

The win also made the Garvey-Lopes-Russell-Cey infield champions at last. "They can do anything they want with us now," Lopes said. "I've got the ring. They can't take that away from me."

Cey was also happy, yet wistful. "Now maybe they won't call us too old. We've been as successful as anybody in the game. We've won four pennants, and now we've won the World Series."

Game 6 was the final game the famed infield played together. Lopes was traded to the Oakland A's after the season.

Perhaps Garvey sensed that this was the end of an era when, while celebrating the title, he said, "There'll really never be another moment like it."

Joe Morgan vs. Terry Forster

Every time I heard Joe Morgan broadcasting a game on TV, I thought about it.

Every time I hear Terry Forster's name mentioned, I think about Sunday, October 3, 1982. The Dodgers vs. the hated Giants. The Dodgers had eliminated the Giants from playoff contention the day before. If they won on Sunday, they would force a one-game playoff against the Atlanta Braves. Fernando was pitching. Easy victory, right?

It should have been, but someone forgot to tell Joe Morgan.

The game was tied 2–2 in the seventh inning when the Dodgers rallied. Consecutive singles by Rick Monday, Ron Cey, and Jose Morales brought Bill Russell to the plate with one out. But Russell struck out, leaving the Dodgers with a tough decision—let Fernando bat, or send up a pinch-hitter and hope he can drive in a couple of runs?

Pitching coach Ron Perranoski asked Fernando how he felt. Fernando pointed to his left shoulder. He meant he was starting to tire, but Perranoski thought he meant his arm hurt.

With that (incorrect) information in hand, manager Tommy Lasorda sent Jorge Orta to pinch-hit. He grounded to second, ending the inning.

"Knowing the type of competitor he was and became, I wish we could have communicated more," Perranoski told the *San Francisco Chronicle* years later. "He was tired but okay. When it happened, there was a lot of second-guessing, but the situation was unknown at the time. We never let on why we pinch-hit for him."

Tom Niedenfuer came in to pitch the bottom of the seventh for the Dodgers and ran into immediate trouble. Bob Brenly singled and Champ Summers doubled, putting runners at second and third with no one out. That was all for Niedenfuer, as he was replaced by Forster, a veteran left-hander who came into the game with 103 career saves.

Forster struck out reliever Greg Minton, who the Giants let bat, and pinch-hitter Jim Wohlford. That brought up Morgan.

Morgan fell behind 1–2 when he unloaded on a slider, sending the ball over the right-field fence for a three-run homer and 5–2 lead.

"I got my A-No. 1 swing at it, and when I hit them that good, they usually go out," Morgan told the *Los Angeles Times* after the game. "I've been in the big leagues 19 years, and I've learned a lot of humility. It's tough to be over there with your head down because you needed to win that last game and you couldn't do it. I have a lot of respect and admiration for the Dodgers. But I wanted this one for the Giants and the fans."

The Dodgers scored one run in the eighth, but that was all.

"I still remember watching Joe between first and second base," teammate Duane Kuiper said in an interview with the *Chronicle* in 1999. "He raised his right arm as if to say, 'If we're not going to win it, you're not, either.'"

Farewell, Steve

Steve Garvey spent 14 seasons in a Dodgers uniform. His father drove the team bus in spring training for years, and Garvey spent time as a bat boy for the team when they played in Vero Beach. He is easily one of the most popular Dodgers of all time.

But it all ended badly.

Garvey was in the final year of his contract in 1982, and the team didn't negotiate a new deal with him during the season. Add in the fact that in Albuquerque, first baseman Greg Brock was busy hitting .310 with 44 homers and 138 RBIs, and you didn't have to be Kreskin to read the writing on the wall—the Dodgers didn't really need Steve Garvey.

While the Dodgers were fighting for a division title, there was a faint tickle at the back of the minds of Dodgers fans—was this the final year for Steve Garvey in a Dodgers uniform?

After the Joe Morgan homer ended the Dodgers' season, all focus turned to Garvey. Would the Dodgers make an attempt to bring him back?

Talks heated up in a two-day period in December. Garvey wanted a five-year deal; the Dodgers wanted to give him three. They were far apart in money. The nervous Dodgers faithful waited.

You have to understand the world in 1982 to realize the anxiousness of Dodgers fans. There was no Internet to get instant updates. There was just your local newscast and your local newspaper. And when it came down to decision time, when the Dodgers and Garvey announced that these two days would make or break a possible deal, the local newscasts went to work. Hourly updates on what was happening. Updates between your favorite shows. The entire front page of the newspapers were devoted to the negotiations. When it was reported that the two sides had agreed on four years, it seemed like a deal would get done.

Then the news came across. Steve Garvey had signed—with the San Diego Padres.

The Padres had offered Garvey five years and $6.6 million. The best the Dodgers would do was four years and $5 million.

What happened?

"They got a good player," Dodgers general manager Al Campanis told the awaiting media after the signing was announced. "We'd like to wish him the best of luck. He's a fine gentleman. I understand he did pretty well monetarily. We made him a good offer, and we had to stay with it. I don't know what he got, but I understand it was better than our offer."

Garvey had his own reaction.

"The last year was like going into a headwind for me. I had to bow my neck and bend my knees and plow forward. I've signed with the San Diego Padres, and that headwind has become a nice breeze at my back."

Looking back now, how did Garvey's departure pay off for both teams?

The Dodgers won the NL West in 1983, with Greg Brock hitting .224 with 20 homers and 66 RBIs, but most fans consider his tenure with the team to be a great disappointment.

The Padres won the NL West in 1984 and went to the World Series. Garvey hit a two-run walk-off homer off stunned Cubs closer Lee Smith in Game 4 of the NLCS that year. In 2012, that hit was voted the most memorable moment in Padres history.

Garvey's number has been retired by the Padres. The Dodgers have not retired his number and apparently never will.

I guess sometimes you can't go home again.

The Greatest Game in Dodger Stadium History

You're probably expecting to read about the Kirk Gibson home run now. Or the four consecutive home runs game. Not yet—we will be talking about those elsewhere. Those were great moments but not the greatest game.

Manager Tommy Lasorda (2) leaps in the air as the team rushes onto the field after winning the game with the Atlanta Braves on Sunday, September 11, 1983, in Los Angeles. The Dodgers scored four runs in the ninth inning to defeat the Braves 7–6. *(AP Photo/Lennox McLendon)*

The greatest game in Dodgers history took place on September 11, 1983. And all you need to do to bring back memories of that game to many longtime fans is say one name: R.J. Reynolds.

The Dodgers began the game with a two-game lead over the Atlanta Braves in the NL West. The Braves just happened to be their opponent that day. Both teams were dragging a bit, having played an extra-inning game the night before. Little did they know they were about to play a 3-hour-and- 48-minute marathon.

"I remember it being really hot that day," said Jim Barrero, a long-time Dodgers fan who was at that game and remembered it vividly during a 2013 interview. "When the Dodgers started to rally, hordes of fans [well, male fans at least] had removed their shirts and were waving them around like rally towels."

After a scoreless first inning, the Dodgers scored twice in the second inning against Len Barker when Jack Fimple, an unsung hero of the 1983 pennant race, doubled to left, scoring Greg Brock and Mike Marshall. Dale Murphy quickly reversed course for the Braves, hitting a three-run homer off Dodgers starter Rick Honeycutt in the top of the third.

Things fell apart further in the fourth as the Braves scored three more runs to make it 6–2. The Dodgers didn't have the greatest offense in the world that year, so it looked very likely that the Braves would be cutting the Dodgers' division lead to one game.

But then a little hope came back into the stadium. With one out in the sixth, Brock walked and Reynolds singled him to second. Rick Monday struck out, and Ken Landreaux walked to load the bases.

That's when the first strange moment of the game came. Atlanta manager Joe Torre (hey, that name sounds familiar) went to the mound and signaled to the bullpen for a left-hander (Terry Forster). Then, realizing the next batter, Steve Sax, was right-handed, Torre changed his mind and signaled for a right-hander. But there was no right-hander warming up.

After some confusion, out of the Braves bullpen came right-hander Tony Brizzolara. He hadn't warmed up, and it showed. He threw four pitches to Sax, none of them near the strike zone, and walked him to force in a run, making it 6–3.

Torre came out again and replaced Brizzolara with Forster, who struck out Bill Russell to end the inning. But that run would prove to be very important.

And then came the bottom of the ninth.

Jose Morales, who looked about 60 years old but was only 38, led off for the Dodgers and doubled off Donnie Moore. Dave Anderson ran for Morales, and Sax walked. That brought Torre out to the mound to bring in the Braves' closer, Gene Garber.

Garber struck out Russell, but Dusty Baker hit a shallow pop fly that fell between Jerry Royster at second and Claudell Washington in right for a single, loading the bases.

That brought up the Dodgers' best hitter, Pedro Guerrero, who teased the Dodger faithful with an at-bat that lasted seven minutes. Strike one. Ball one. Grounder just foul. Ball two. Ground foul. Fouled into the stands. Ground foul.

While all this was going on, the fans in the Stadium were on their feet, cheering every move, and dying just a little bit every time a ball was foul by inches.

Ball three. Full count, bases loaded. One out. 6–3 Braves. Bottom of the ninth. Garber vs. Guerrero.

Then it was ball four. That made it 6–4 Braves as the Dodgers were seemingly using slow torture on their fans, playing station-to-station ball and scoring as slowly as possible.

That brought up Mike Marshall and strange moment No. 2.

Marshall didn't waste any time, hitting a long fly ball to right that looked like an easy play for Washington. Except the sun got in the way, and Washington lost the ball. Two runs scored as Marshall pulled into second for a double.

Garber then walked Brock intentionally to load the bases.

Up to the plate strolled R.J. Reynolds. It was 6–6, still one out, bottom of the ninth. A victory would put a dagger into the heart of the Braves and give the Dodgers a three-game lead in the NL West.

Ball one.

Reynolds looked down to third-base coach Joey Amalfitano, but no one was looking for a squeeze play. The bases were loaded, so it was a force out at home. Plus, all Reynolds needed to do was hit a long fly ball and the game was over.

Garber pitched, and Reynolds laid down a perfect bunt. It rolled down the first-base line. The first baseman was nowhere near the ball, and by the time Garber recovered and rushed over to grab it, Guerrero was crossing home plate. The Dodgers won, and it was pandemonium at Dodger Stadium. R.J. Reynolds was a hero.

"I forget where our original seats were that day, but as young people used to do back then, we moved around all game to get better and better seats," Barrero said. "I think by the time the ninth inning came, we were in the loge level behind the Dodgers dugout so we had a great view of the winning play. When Reynolds made his bunt and the play proved successful, this feeling of chills went through my body [ironic because it was so hot that day]. It was a surge that I have felt few other times at a live sporting event."

A lot of fans thought there was some sort of heavenly influence on the outcome. They may have been right.

"It also was 'Nuns Day' that day at Dodger Stadium," Barrero said, "and I remember thinking to myself, *How appropriate that the Dodgers pulled off this miraculous win because it was some kind of divine intervention for them to win the way they did.* It was quite a sight, seeing all these baseball-loving nuns jumping up and down in their habits."

It was the greatest game ever played at Dodger Stadium.

"In the aftermath of the win," Barrero said, "with the crowd going nuts, many of the fans looked up toward the press box where Vin Scully, in the excitement of the moment, was on his feet as well and he had this look of glee on his face that I'll never forget. I never realized how important it was to him when the Dodgers did well. Scully was giving the thumbs-up sign to everyone and even clenched and pumped his fist a few times as he smiled and connected with the fans. Another moment I will never forget, and one of the many reasons why I love the man so much."

If you doubt this was the greatest game in Dodger Stadium history, find a Dodgers fan who has been a fan since before 1983. Say the name R.J. Reynolds to them.

Then watch for the smile.

Ozzie and Jack

After a mediocre 1984 season, the Dodgers rebounded to win the NL West in 1985 and played the St. Louis Cardinals in the NL Championship Series.

The Dodgers won Games 1 and 2 at home and seemed to be World Series bound. This was the first year that the Championship Series in both leagues was a best-of-seven instead of a best-of-five, so the Cardinals could still lose one more game and stay alive.

They didn't lose again.

The Cardinals won Games 3 and 4 to set up a pivotal Game 5 in St. Louis. With the score tied 2–2 in the bottom of the ninth, the Dodgers brought in their closer, Tom Niedenfuer, who retired Willie McGee on a pop fly to third to start the inning.

That brought up Ozzie Smith. Smith was the greatest defensive shortstop in baseball history, but he wasn't known for his bat. He certainly wasn't known for his power. The switch-hitting Smith batted left-handed against Niedenfuer, and it was quickly pointed out during the broadcast that Smith had never hit a home run batting left-handed during his entire eight-season major league career to that point.

Smith decided the time was ripe to change that.

On a 1–2 pitch, Smith lined a ball down the right-field line that barely cleared the fence for an improbable home run and a 3–2 Cardinals victory.

In 2005, Cardinals fans voted Smith's homer as the greatest moment in Busch Stadium history.

"What can you do? It happened," Niedenfuer said in a 2010 interview. "Looking back on it, it's a very proud feeling that your manager had enough confidence in you to be the guy he put in that situation. I wouldn't trade it for anything in the world because I loved being out there. But when it happened, all I could think was I let the team down.

"The pitch was down and in instead of up and in. And when you see the highlights, it cleared the fence by about 6"."

But Niedenfuer wasn't done giving up memorable home runs in that series.

Game 6 was back at Dodger Stadium. The Dodgers took a 5–4 lead in the bottom of the eighth thanks to a solo home run from Mike Marshall. Niedenfuer, who relieved Orel Hershiser in the seventh inning, was on the mound again in the top of the ninth. After striking out Cesar Cedeno, he gave up a single to McGee and walked Smith. Tommy Herr grounded to first, putting runners on second and third with two out and the Cardinals' most dangerous hitter, Jack Clark, due up.

It seemed to be a situation that demanded an intentional walk. Manager Tommy Lasorda didn't order one, though. On the first pitch, Clark homered over the left-field fence, giving the Cardinals a 7–5 lead and ripping the heart out of the Dodgers, who went down meekly in the bottom of the ninth as the Cardinals advanced to the World Series.

To this day, Lasorda defends his decision not to walk Clark and criticizes all the second-guessers. "A second-guesser is someone who doesn't know anything about the first guess. And the second-guesser is someone who needs two guesses to be right."

Lacking Some Necessities

Al Campanis was general manager of the Dodgers from 1968 until April 6, 1987, when he was done in by his own words.

To celebrate the 40th anniversary of Jackie Robinson breaking the color barrier, the ABC news show *Nightline* devoted a show that was to feature former Dodgers great Don Newcombe; Campanis, who had roomed with Robinson when both played for the Dodgers; and Roger Kahn, author of the celebrated *Boys of Summer* book that detailed the Robinson-era Dodgers.

The show was a logistical nightmare. Newcombe's plane was delayed, and he missed the show entirely. Kahn got stuck in traffic because of local floods and was a few minutes late arriving, and the Dodgers were in Houston, leaving ABC with only one option if they wanted Campanis on the show—he would have to sit in a chair at home plate and appear live via satellite.

The show began with Campanis in Houston and *Nightline* host Ted Koppel in ABC Studios in New York. The sight of Campanis sitting in the middle of the cavernous Astrodome, with all the lights turned out except for a lone TV light illuminating him at home plate, was spooky. He appeared to be coming to you live from the bottom of a dark pit, which seemed pretty appropriate, all things considered.

Before they went to Campanis, they showed Rachel Robinson, in a taped interview, saying, "It's not coincidental that baseball in the 40-year period has not been able to integrate at any other level other than the players' level…we have a long way to go."

There were a few comments from Koppel, Kahn, and Campanis about Robinson before Koppel referred back to Rachel Robinson's statement about there being few African Americans at the executive level in baseball.

Here is the transcript:

Koppel: Mr. Campanis, you're an old friend of Jackie Robinson's. You're still in baseball. Why is it that there are no black managers, no black general managers, no black owners?

Campanis: Well, Mr. Koppel, there have been some black managers, but I really can't answer that question directly. The only thing I can say is that you have to pay your dues when you become a manager. Generally, you have to go to minor leagues. There's not very much pay involved, and some of the better known black players have been able to get into other fields and make a pretty good living in that way.

Koppel: Yeah, but you know in your heart of hearts—and we're going to take a break for a commercial—you know that that's a lot of baloney.

105

I mean, there are a lot of black players, there are a lot of great black baseball men who would dearly love to be in managerial positions, and I guess what I'm really asking you is to, you know, peel it away a little bit. Just tell me, why you think it is. Is there still that much prejudice in baseball today?

Campanis: No, I don't believe it's prejudice. I truly believe that they may not have some of the necessities to be, let's say, a field manager, or perhaps a general manager.

Koppel: Do you really believe that?

Campanis: Well, I don't say that all of them, but they certainly are short. How many quarterbacks do you have? How many pitchers do you have that are black?

Koppel: Yeah, but I mean, I gotta tell you, that sounds like the same kind of garbage we were hearing 40 years ago about players, when they were saying, "Aah, not really—not really cut out. Remember the days, you know, hit a black football player in the knees, and you know, no…" That really sounds like garbage, if—if you'll forgive me for saying so."

Campanis: No, it's not—it's not garbage, Mr. Koppel, because I played on a college team, and the center fielder was black, and the backfield at NYU, with a fullback who was black, never knew the difference, whether he was black or white, we were teammates. So it just might just be—why are black men, or black people, not good swimmers? Because they don't have the buoyancy.

Koppel: Oh, I don't—I don't—it may just be that they don't have access to all the country clubs and the pools. But I'll tell you what, let's take a break, and we'll continue our discussion in a moment.

The response from the public was immediate—outrage. Al Campanis resigned two days later, forever painted as a racist. Whether that is fair or unfair is not for me to say, but perhaps Harry Edwards, a sociologist and civil-rights leader whom baseball hired in the wake of Campanis' comments to find ways to increase diversity in baseball's executive ranks, said it best in a 2012 ESPN interview.

"He didn't get a raw deal," Edwards said of Campanis. "He got the deal he ordered up, but he was one of the most honorable men in the whole process and he handled it with class, with conscientiousness, and with courage."

Replacing Al Campanis

Going unnoticed by many in the continuing furor over Campanis' words was Fred Claire, the man who replaced him as Dodgers GM.

Claire was the Dodgers' vice president of public relations before being promoted to general manager, which seems appropriate considering he was walking into a public-relations nightmare, replacing the man being vilified as a racist by many across the country and in baseball. But Claire tried to put all that aside to focus on the task at hand.

"My main thought in replacing Al Campanis was that we needed to get the baseball organization—major leagues, minor leagues, and scouting—back on track," Claire said in a 2013 interview. "We had been through a very tough time, and it was important to establish the change in leadership."

Claire was so busy in his new role that he didn't really have time to think about the tumult surrounding him.

"Other than feeling sad for Al, it was not a difficult transition for me in that I had been with the Dodgers for nearly 20 years when I became the GM and had worked closely with all of the people in baseball operations.

"I had attended GM meetings with Al and had been involved with the agents, other teams, and all of the parties I would have to deal with."

Claire was taking over one of the most storied franchises in history, on the fly, at the start of the season. This could have been a prime target for other GMs in baseball, who could have seen a newcomer ripe for the picking. Maybe lure a prized prospect from Claire for an over-the-hill player. But that was far from the case.

"The other GMs, many of them friends for nearly two decades, were great to me," Claire said. "Frank Cashen, Harry Dalton, Roland Hemond, Sandy Alderson, John Schuerholtz, Al Rosen, Syd Thrift, Gene Michael, Pat Gillick, Hank Peters, Dallas Green, and so many others were wonderful and receptive and great in every way."

And it wasn't long before Claire made his first move, one that paid immediate and long-range dividends.

Mickey

No, not Mantle. Hatcher.

The first move Claire made when he became general manager was to bring back an old favorite, Mickey Hatcher.

"I signed Mickey as a free agent on my second day on the job because Bill Madlock had to go on the DL and I knew Mickey from his previous time with the Dodgers," Claire said in a 2013 interview. "I knew Mickey was the type of player I wanted to add; he had great enthusiasm and was a quality person."

Hatcher paid immediate dividends, getting the game-winning single in his first game and hitting .282 with seven homers and 42 RBIs with the Dodgers in 1987.

But it was 1988 when he really proved his worth.

Hatcher was the leader of "The Stuntmen," which was what the bench of that World Series team called itself. Every time a player went down, there was a Stuntman ready to fill the hole. Need a key pinch-hit? Call on a Stuntman: Mickey Hatcher, Rick Dempsey, Dave Anderson, and Tracy Woodson. It didn't matter what you needed, one of them would step up.

Mickey Hatcher celebrates his two-run first-inning home run against the Oakland A's in the first game of the 1988 World Series at Dodger Stadium in Los Angeles on October 15, 1988. *(AP Photo/John Swart)*

But not even the Stuntmen would believe the extra mile Hatcher went in the 1988 World Series. All he had to do was fill in for the injured Kirk Gibson, the Dodgers' leader and league MVP.

Hatcher's first at-bat of Game 1 was a home run. And Hatcher circled the bases in about 10 seconds, or as Joe Garagiola said while calling the game on NBC, "He ran so fast it was like he was afraid they would take the home run away before he crossed home plate."

Hatcher hit .368 with two homers and five RBIs in the Series, and many thought he should have been named Series MVP instead of Orel Hershiser.

"As far as credit, I don't think Mickey ever thought about that for any moment of his career," Claire said. "He was and is the ultimate team player, someone who loves the game and gives the game everything he has at all times. He did that as a player, he did that as a coach, and he will do that as long as he puts on a uniform."

So it was no surprise that he stepped up big when the Dodgers needed him most.

"I knew Mickey could help us because I knew Mickey," Claire said. "There never ever was a doubt in my mind."

The Kirk Gibson Home Run Calls

The Kirk Gibson home run in Game 1 of the 1988 World Series is one of the most iconic plays in baseball history and was voted the greatest moment in L.A. sports history by the L.A. Sports Council in 2000. Books, essays, and poems have been written about it, but most Dodgers fans remember it in one of three ways because there happened to be three outstanding play-by-play calls of the at-bat. On NBC, Vin Scully and Joe Garagiola called it. On CBS Radio, Jack Buck and Bill White handled it. And on KABC Radio in Los Angeles, Don Drysdale made the call. People still quote all three, depending on which one they were listening to. Each call is great in its own way, and below is each call, starting with Scully and Garagiola.

To set the scene, Mike Scioscia popped out to start the bottom of the ninth. Jeff Hamilton struck out. Mike Davis walked, bringing Gibson to the plate. Dennis Eckersely was the A's pitcher, and Ron Hassey the catcher.

Here is the NBC call just after Davis walked.

Scully: "And look who's coming up."

(There is a 36-second pause while the crowd cheers and we can hear the PA announcer say Gibson's name in the background.)

Scully: "All year long, they looked to him to light the fire, and all year long, he answered the demands until he was physically unable to start tonight, with two bad legs. The bad left hamstring, and the

Kirk Gibson raises his arm in celebration as he rounds the bases after hitting a game-winning two-run home run in the bottom of the ninth inning to beat the Oakland A's 5–4 in the first game of the World Series at Dodger Stadium on October 15, 1988. *(AP Photo/Rusty Kennedy)*

swollen right knee. And, with two out, you talk about a roll of the dice...this is it."

Scully: "If he hits the ball on the ground, I would imagine he would be running at 50 percent. So the Dodgers, trying to catch lightning right now."

At this point, Eckersley delivered his first pitch.

Scully: "Fouled away.... He was complaining about the fact that with the left knee bothering him he can't push off. Well, now he can't push off and he can't land."

Garagiola: "He's gotta use all arms. Look at this crowd, on its feet. Quite a tribute."

Scully: "Four three A's. Ninth inning. Not a bad opening act."

At this point, Eckersley threw to first to try to pick off Mike Davis.

Scully: "Mike Davis, by the way, has stolen seven out of 10 if you are wondering about Lasorda throwing the dice again."

There is a seven-second pause as Eckersley turned his attention to Gibson again.

Scully: "0 and one."

Eckersley pitched.

Scully: "Fouled away again."

Garagiola: "And he's staying on that outside corner. He's not going to give him a ball to pull. With Davis he just missed, but here's two quick strikes, both fastballs that kind of tailed away to the outside corner. Hassey has not even flirted with the inside part of the plate."

At this point, the NBC cameras focused on the A's dugout, and Coach Dave Duncan made a gesture with his hands.

Scully: "You saw Dave Duncan gesturing, he was gesturing to Carney Lansford at third."

Eckersley was ready to make his next pitch.

Scully: "0 and two to Gibson. The infield is back with two out and Davis at first."

Eckersley threw to first.

Scully: "Now Gibson, during the year, not necessarily in this spot, but he was a threat to bunt. No way tonight. No wheels."

Garagiola: "They're plenty deep in the outfield. They are playing him straight away to center field. Right down the line."

Eckersley threw to first again, and Garagiola made a comment on Davis possibly stealing second.

Garagiola: "He's a threat now with two strikes."

There is a 12-second pause as the crowd started cheering louder and Eckersley prepared to pitch.

Scully: "No balls and two strikes. Two out."

Gibson hit a weak grounder to first that trickled just foul.

Scully: "Little nubber.... Foul."

Gibson was a quarter of the way to first base and turned around to return to the plate.

Scully: "And it had to be an effort to run that far. Gibson was so banged up that he was not introduced. He did not come out onto the field before the game."

NBC showed a replay of Gibson's weak grounder that went foul.

Garagiola: "You can really see the limp. He's not driving that ball at all. It was by him. You can see he almost has to talk to his legs and say, 'Hey, let's go, we've got to get out of here.'"

Scully: "It's one thing to favor one leg, but you can't favor two."

Garagiola: "No way. And that's what he's trying to do. He really is."

Eckersley pitched again.

Scully: "0 and two to Gibson. Ball one."

Hassey makes a snap throw to first to try to pick off Davis.

Scully: "And a throw down to first! Davis just did get back. Good play by Ron Hassey, using Gibson as a screen. He took a shot at the runner, and Mike Davis didn't see it for that split-second and that made it close."

Garagiola: "A lot of times what you will do is you'll give a sign to the first baseman that says, 'Now be there.' They call it the Now Be There play. If I get the ball, I'm going to throw it."

Eckersley got ready to pitch, and Garagiola continued, "Fourteen fastballs in a row. That's all he has been throwing."

While Garagiola was talking, Davis took off for second as the pitch came to Gibson. Scully had to hurry and interrupt Garagiola.

Scully: "There goes Davis! And it's fouled away.... So Mike Davis, who has stolen seven out of 10 and carrying the tying run, was on the move."

Garagiola: "They want to give Gibson a good shot at it with two strikes, but with two strikes, Davis a threat as we said, hoping a bloop hit will score that big run."

Eckersley prepared to pitch.

Scully: "Gibson shaking his left leg, making it quiver like a horse trying to get rid of a troublesome fly."

The pitch by Eckersley is outside.

Scully: "Two and two."

NBC showed a shot of the Dodgers' dugout, focusing on Mike Scioscia.

Scully: "Mike Scioscia can only sit now and sweat it out. He led off the inning and popped up."

NBC turned to the A's dugout and manager Tony La Russa.

Scully: "Tony La Russa. One out away from win No. 1."

Eckersley was ready to pitch.

Garagiola: "Here's the big pitch. He's gotta make it happen on this one."

Instead, Eckersley threw to first again.

Scully: "Two balls and two strikes with two out."

Garagiola: "Those extra steps that Davis will get if the count goes to three and two are very big. So Hassey and Eckersley want that pitch of decision right here."

Eckersley pitched, and Davis took off for second.

Scully: "There he goes. WAY outside, and he's stolen it."

Garagiola: "Hassey starts to throw and kind of bumps Gibson, but it was way too late. Davis was way down there, almost as if he could have walked in."

NBC showed a replay of the pitch and stolen base.

Garagiola: "Not a bad pitch to handle for Hassey. Outside. Now watch when he starts to throw, he bumps Gibson. And Harvey says, 'No, no. He had the base stolen.'"

Scully: "So Mike Davis, the tying run, is at second base with two out. Now the Dodgers don't need the muscle of Gibson as much as a base hit. And on deck is the leadoff man, Steve Sax."

Eckersley was ready to pitch.

Scully: "Three and two."

Gibson asked for time and stepped out of the batter's box. There was an 11-second pause as Scully just let the noise of the crowd fill the microphone.

Scully: "Sax waiting on deck. But the game right now is at the plate."

Eckersley pitched. Gibson swung.

Scully: "High fly ball into right field.... She is...GONE!"

Scully remained quiet for one minute and nine seconds as Dodger Stadium erupted into pandemonium. He finally broke the quiet with one of the great lines of all time.

Scully: "In a year that has been so improbable, the impossible has happened."

NBC replayed the home run and showed Gibson limping around the bases.

Scully: "And now, the only question was, could he make it around the base paths unassisted?"

There was another 20-second pause.

Scully: "You know, I said it once before, a few days ago, that Kirk Gibson was not the Most Valuable Player, that the Most Valuable Player for the Dodgers was Tinkerbell. But tonight, I think Tinkerbell backed off for Kirk Gibson."

NBC showed a great reaction shot of Eckersley looking devastated.

Scully: "And look at Eckersley—shocked to his toes! They are going wild at Dodger Stadium—no one wants to leave!"

Over on CBS Radio, longtime Cardinals announcer Jack Buck and Bill White were calling the game. Instead of focusing on the whole at-bat, here are Buck's great words about the homer.

Buck: "We have a big three two pitch coming here from Eckersley. Gibson swings, and a fly ball to deep right field! This is gonna be a home run! Unbelievable! A home run for Gibson! And the Dodgers have won the game, five to four; I don't believe what I just saw! I don't believe what I just saw! Is this really happening, Bill?"

Buck ended it with:

"One of the most remarkable finishes to any World Series game...a one-handed home run by Kirk Gibson! And the Dodgers have won it...five to four; and I'm stunned, Bill. I have seen a lot of dramatic finishes in a lot of sports, but this one might top almost every other one."

If you ask people who heard it live, they will tell you that Drysdale's call topped them all. It's extremely hard to find Drysdale's call of the entire at-bat, but his call of the home run itself is legendary for the level of excitement in his voice.

Drysdale: "Well, the crowd on its feet and if there was ever a preface to 'Casey at the Bat,' it would have to be the ninth inning. Two out. The tying run aboard, the winning run at the plate, and Kirk Gibson standing at the plate. Gibson, a deep sigh...re-gripping the bat...shoulders just shrugged...now goes to the top of the helmet, as he always does... steps in with that left foot. Eckersley, working out of the stretch...here's the three-two pitch—and a drive hit to right field [voice changes to high pitch] WAY BACK! THIS BALL...IS GONE! [After a 23-second delay] This crowd will not stop! They can't believe the ending! And this time, Mighty Casey did NOT strike out!"

The Streak

Orel Hershiser didn't look much like a pitcher. He was thin and wore glasses. He made Clark Kent look like a pro wrestler. But an amazing thing happened when he took the mound.

In 1983, Dodgers manager Tommy Lasorda was looking for a way to instill some confidence in the young Hershiser, who he felt had all the physical tools but lacked the mental toughness to last in the majors.

"I don't like your name," Lasorda told Hershiser. "From now on, your name is Bulldog. You're going to act like a bulldog and pitch like a bulldog."

The nickname seemed to work.

"I changed his life," Lasorda said. "When a batter comes up, he's saying, 'I can't wait to face a guy whose name is Orel.' But now he's going to say, 'He must be a tough pitcher to have a name like Bulldog.'"

From 1984 to 1989, Hershiser was the Dodgers' best pitcher and one of the best pitchers in baseball, compiling a 98–64 record with a 2.68 ERA. And he turned in a truly magical season in 1988.

No one expected the Dodgers to contend for the NL West title that season. They were coming off two seasons in which they finished under .500 and were picked by most experts to finish fourth in 1988. But they moved into the division lead on May 25 and were never out of first place after that.

Heading into the final stretch of the season, Hershiser made sure the team stayed in first. He put on a command performance, pitching 59 consecutive scoreless innings and five consecutive shutouts.

Orel Hershiser winds up for a pitch against the San Diego Padres in San Diego, California, on Wednesday, September 28, 1988. Hershiser broke Don Drysdale's 58.2 scoreless innings record when he threw a scoreless 10th inning and set the new mark at 59 innings. *(AP Photo/Lenny Ignelzi)*

"I caught 16 pitchers who won the Cy Young Award, and I never caught anyone who pitched like him that year," Dodgers catcher Rick Dempsey said. "We knew when he was pitching that the game was over." Here is a quick look at the shutouts.

The first shutout in the streak was a 3–0 win over the Atlanta Braves on September 5, 1988. The game was notable for the fact Hershiser struck out two-time league MVP Dale Murphy four times, the only time in Murphy's 2,180-game career in which he struck out four times in a game against the same pitcher.

On September 10, Hershiser beat the Cincinnati Reds 5–0, not only getting his second consecutive shutout but also picking up his 20th victory of the season.

On September 14, the Braves got another chance at him but fared no better, losing 1–0.

On September 19, it was another 1–0 win, this time against Houston.

"One of the things that helped me get the streak was that the offense wasn't scoring many runs," Hershiser said in a 2013 interview. "When your team is winning big, you trade outs for runs a lot, but early in the streak, I couldn't."

On September 23, it looked like the streak would end.

In the third inning against San Francisco, Hershiser got into a little trouble. Jose Uribe led off with a single and moved to second on Atlee Hammaker's infield hit. Brett Butler grounded to second, but the Dodgers were unable to turn the double play, putting runners on first and third with one out.

Ernest Riles came to the plate and hit a grounder to second. Steve Sax fed Alfredo Griffin to force Butler at second, but the throw to first was too late and the run scored.

The streak was over at 42 innings.

Except it wasn't.

First-base umpire Paul Runge ruled that Butler had drifted too far right of the base on his slide and interfered with Griffin's throw. He called Riles out—so no run scored, the inning was over, and the streak continued.

"For something like this to happen," Hershiser said, "you have to catch one break."

Even now, Butler says Runge blew the call. "That was the only time in 17 years that that's ever happened to me," Butler told the *Los Angeles Times.* "I'd done it the same way for all those years."

The play brought to mind a similar play that kept Drysdale's streak alive. With his streak at 45 innings in 1968, Drysdale faced a bases-loaded situation against the Giants. Dick Dietz was the batter, and he was hit by a Drysdale fastball, seemingly forcing in a run and ending Drysdale's streak.

However, plate umpire Harry Wendelstedt ruled that Dietz had not tried to avoid the pitch. He was ordered back to the plate, and Drysdale retired him on a fly ball to preserve the streak.

With the streak at 49 innings, Hershiser made his final start of the season against the San Diego Padres. It looked like the best he could do was tie Drysdale, unless by some miracle the game went into extra innings tied at 0–0. But what were the odds of that happening?

Pretty good, actually.

Hershiser shut out the Padres for nine innings to tie the record, but the Dodgers failed to score against Andy Hawkins, sending the game to extra innings tied at 0–0. One problem, though. Hershiser did not want to go out for the 10th inning. He wanted to go into the record books tied with Drysdale.

"I loved it because he had so much respect for Don Drysdale," Lasorda said. "That was the thing he was concerned with. He just needed someone to push him a little bit. I told him, 'Get out there and break it.'"

Hershiser pitched a scoreless 10th to break the record and came out of the game, which the Padres won 2–1 in 16 innings.

"I felt wonderful for Hershiser," Vin Scully said. "And I thought we were blessed. I mean, what a set of circumstances to have the man whose record is broken part of the same group with the man who broke it. That was, to me, kind of a special moment."

Amazingly, opponents went 0-for-31 with runners in scoring position and 0-for-9 with runners on third base during Hershiser's streak. It is one of the great moments in baseball history, and it is just the kind of record you would expect a guy named Bulldog to have.

The Gibson Homer in His Own Words

Kirk Gibson was kind enough to offer his thoughts on his most memorable moment from the 1988 season, including what went through his mind during the iconic Game 1 homer.

The most memorable moment of the season?

"When we won the World Series, celebrating in that small Oakland locker room and on the plane back to L.A. Because when you do that, along the way, I don't know who picked us that year. Probably nobody. So we always felt like we were against the odds. Then you get closer and closer and closer, and you're scared things are going to turn on you the wrong way and they never did. Just getting that last out right there, knowing that it was real."

What he was thinking during the home run?

"First of all, it was like almost some kind of a foolish thing to really go up there and hit just because of the shape I was in. Just really sitting there in the clubhouse and almost dreaming about doing it, then to go up there and do it, it was like, 'Can you believe it?'

"I remember when I was rounding the bases, my parents went through my mind. Throughout my career, there were a lot of doubters, a lot of people who directed a lot of criticism at me. People would say things to my dad, and initially, early in my career, they had to defend me.

I told them, 'You guys don't have to defend me. I'm going to bust it, and I'm going to fail sometimes. But we'll have a laugh some day that it will all be worth it.' When I did it, I thought, *This is the moment.*

"Literally as I was rounding the bases, past second base. When I got to home plate I remember thinking, *You guys don't jump on me,* because I was hurting. I was like, 'No, no,' but it didn't matter.

"Then right at the end of the game when I went in, I think it was Bob Costas, he wanted me to go right on TV. I said, 'No,' because I wanted to go in and celebrate with my teammates. I walked in and everybody waited. Then jumped around. Then I went back out and did the interview with Bob Costas, I believe. It was on the scoreboard. I went out there five to 10 minutes later, and nobody had left."

The Gibson Homer: What Were They Thinking?

Kirk Gibson has given dozens of interviews about his Game 1 homer, but what were his teammates thinking when the ball soared over the right-field fence? I asked many of the players on the 1988 team what their favorite moment from the season was, and what they were thinking when Gibson hit his homer.

Dave Anderson, infielder

Season: "Kirk Gibson's home run."

Gibson homer: "We were going to win the World Series."

Tim Belcher, pitcher

Season: "Several things stand out. Steve Sax starting the season with a home run, I believe on the first pitch in the bottom of the first inning. Gibson scoring from second base on a passed ball more than once. Orel's streak and the nine inning scoreless tie in San Diego that made breaking the record possible. Don Drysdale. And, without a doubt, the Gibson home run in Game 1 of the World Series.

Gibson homer: "Thanks Gibby! I just spit the hook for what would have been a World Series loss." (Belcher was the Game 1 starter.)

Alfredo Griffin, shortstop

Season: "Without question, Kirk Gibson's home run. Davis pinch-hit for me, he walked, stole second, and that was it, Kirk hit the home run, I was just jumping around like crazy."

Gibson homer: "That was incredible. Oakland was playing good, was winning the game, that changed everything around. It was amazing."

Mickey Hatcher, infielder-outfielder

Season: "God, there were too many of them...it was one of those things that when you look back on the season, you realize how many guys contributed in so many ways, when it was all said and done, all the things that happened that season to get us there and to win, some of the Kirk Gibson at-bats to Mike Scioscia at-bats to Jeff Hamilton's at-bats to Orel Hershiser, the way he pitched—think we had three different pitchers win a game with the bat during the season—you look at all that and you realize what it takes to be a world champion. Those are the things that I think about."

Gibson homer: "It was just unbelievable. Davis stole second, I think everybody right there thought Gibby had a chance to get a base hit and tie the game. That's what we were looking at. Before that, we were watching him battle through it, but when Davis stole second, everyone kind of felt something might happen here, that we might be able to get that run, we just hope he can get to first base. Then when he hit that ball in the seats, that was just unbelievable."

Orel Hershiser, pitcher

Season: "The last out of the World Series, Tony Phillips striking out on a fastball in. It's like having your first child. It's like walking down the aisle.

123

It's the happiest feeling you can have in your life. You see your mom and dad in the stands and think, *This is something you gave me the opportunity to do.*"

Gibson homer: "I was jumping up and down, but as I was celebrating, I was thinking, *I've got to pitch Game 2.*"

Ricky Horton, relief pitcher

Season: "Pitching in a playoff game in New York."

Gibson homer: "My initial thought was, *Is Tommy out of his mind?* Then, *I hope Jesse Orosco does not drop me!* He was carrying me around the bullpen after the home run!"

Tim Leary, pitcher

Season: "For me personally, it was when I got called in to pinch hit in the 11th inning of a game in August against the Giants and I got a hit. It was a tie game. Mike Davis was on the bench on the top step, arguing a call with Paul Runge, and Paul Runge threw him out of the game. They walked the No. 8 batter to get to me with the bases loaded and two out. I got the count to 3–2 and hit the ball up the middle. It was a special game against the Giants. The last night, I had pitched and won."

Gibson homer: "I was the first relief pitcher in that game. I was in the clubhouse in shorts and shower shoes. When I the count got to 3–2, the scouting report was, 'Look for the backdoor slider.' We knew it was coming. When he hit it, I jumped up, put on my uniform pants and shirt, and ran out to the field. For an hour, no one could sit down. It was the most incredible excitement ever. We had Hershiser pitching the next day. We tore their hearts. It was like we won the World Series right there. It was more exciting, actually, than winning Game 5."

Mike Marshall, right fielder

Season: "Too many to name. Leary's pinch-hit game winner. Gibby scoring from second base on a wild pitch. Orel's streak."

Gibson homer: "Not as surprised as everyone else. Just when you think you've seen it all the improbable happens. The longer you live, the more amazing things happen."

Steve Sax, second baseman

Season: "There were so many things. Orel breaking Drysdale's record. Gibson winning the MVP. Mike Scioscia's home run off Gooden. Also, Gibson, in the rain against New York, a catch on a ball that would've been disastrous for us. He made a tremendous catch. He was playing in shallow left field. Someone hit a ball behind him to his right. He slipped and fell, but he was able to make a catch. John Shelby made a couple of huge plays in center field, as well. Our outfielders made some huge plays."

Gibson homer: "I was the next guy up, so I had a good view of it. We weren't the most talented team, but we were the best team. The Mets beat us 10-of-11 times, and beating them in the NLCS was a huge accomplishment. So when Gibson hit the home run, it seemed like it was time for us to win it. Big things were happening after big things."

Mike Scioscia, catcher

Season: "There wasn't really one moment, it was almost like a rolling thunder momentum thing through whole season. We only had two big-name players [Gibson, Hershiser], and there were some personal accomplishments there with Kirk getting the MVP and Orel going 59 scoreless innings, but just the feeling that a team was in sync, there were guys who would platoon, there were guys who played every day, there were matchups that were used in given situations, our bullpen was by committee, don't think there was one moment where you went, 'Wow!' until you clinched.

Gibson homer: "It was funny, but it was surreal the way that situation unraveled. It was just like the poem, 'Casey at the Bat,' that's something that never happens, you never have the hometown slugger come up in a situation like that and hit the home run. I can't ever remember that happening. Other guys have hit home runs, but it's not usually the hometown slugger. It was surreal the way he was able to play, the whole setting, everything from the scouting report about the back-door slider, a lot of things went through my head at the time he was up to the bat, when the count got there, it was unbelievable the way everything came together."

John Shelby, center fielder

Season: "It's really hard to pinpoint one thing. We were a very close-knit ballclub. We did the itty-bitty things. Like my walk and Scioscia coming up and getting the big two-run home run (in the ninth inning of Game 4 of the NLCS against the Mets). The Mets felt like they had that one put away. But after I drew the walk and Scioscia hit a two-run home run to tie it, that gave us a lot of momentum. We never gave up. Little things like my drawing the walk kept us in the ballgame and gave us a chance. We always felt like someone on the club was doing something. We even had pitchers come up and get hits for us."

Gibson homer: "Knowing his condition, realizing the way he fouled off a couple pitches, it didn't look pretty. But deep down inside, all we could do was hope. And he hit the home run. If he had hit anything but a home run, he probably would've been thrown out. When he hit the ball, everyone was wide-eyed. It wasn't hit real high. It was kind of on a line. It went back and back, and all of a sudden the whole place exploded. When it happens, your mind goes wild."

Franklin Stubbs, first base

Season: "Jesse Orosco put some black stuff in Gibson's helmet in spring training. Gibson didn't play that day because he said we played around too much. I realized at that time that we had a chance to win. It was in the first week of games at Vero Beach."

Gibson homer: "I still remember Mel Didier saying that if the count was 3–2, Eckersley would throw a backdoor slider. That's what he said. The main thing was that Mike Davis stole second base because I knew Gibby couldn't run. I said, 'Here it comes.' I didn't think he could get around on a fastball, but I thought he could get around on a slider. I was thinking, *We got Game 1. We've got three more to finish the deal.* When you're a little kid, all you dream about is playing in a World Series and winning. You can't explain it."

Tracy Woodson, infielder

Season: "Gibby's homer. I knew at that moment that we were winning it all. I think the ball landed in one of the terminals at LAX!"

Gibson homer: "I couldn't believe it. I still have it on tape and play it when I'm recruiting players to come to play for me." (Woodson is the head coach at the University of Richmond.)

Some fans think the Dodgers made some sort of supernatural deal to win the World Series in 1988. The team added fuel to that fire by going the next two decades without even making the World Series.

Ross Porter, Marathon Man

When you work alongside Vin Scully, it is easy to be overlooked. But if you ask Dodgers fans today to name any Dodgers announcer in history other than Scully, odds are that they will say the name of Ross Porter.

Porter was a broadcaster, analyst, and postgame talk show host for the Dodgers from 1977 to 2004. Usually, he would share the booth with a couple of broadcast partners, be it Scully, Jerry Doggett, or Don Drysdale. They would split up the innings depending on if the game was on TV, radio, or both, each taking turns calling the action.

On August 23, 1989, Porter found himself alone in the broadcast booth. No big deal, Ross Porter could call nine innings of game action in his sleep. By the time that day's game against the Montreal Expos ended, he almost was calling the game in his sleep.

Porter was kind enough to share his recollections of that game.

The Dodgers had already completed series in Philadelphia and New York and were finishing their Eastern road trip with three games at Montreal.

Vin Scully worked the first two series but flew home instead of making the trip to Canada. Don Drysdale was on hand for the first two games at Olympic Stadium, but on the morning of August 23, he learned his wife, Annie, was in labor and about to have a baby. Don immediately booked a flight to Los Angeles and left before the final game of the road trip.

There was no telecast that night. It was radio only. My wife, Lin, was on the trip so she sat with me in the Dodgers broadcast booth, reading a book.

In the booth to my left were the French-speaking Expos announcers. To my right were the Spanish-speaking Dodgers broadcasters. I was the only English-speaking play-by-play announcer describing the action.

Two months earlier, the Dodgers had been involved in a 22-inning game at Houston, which the Astros won. Don had the night off, so Vin and I had that one to ourselves on radio and television.

One season after winning the World Series, the Dodgers did not fare well in 1989. They would finish six games under .500 and in fourth place, 14 games behind.

In their last game in Montreal that year, the Dodgers received excellent pitching. So did the Expos. The game was scoreless for nine, 12, and 15 innings. At one point, Lin asked me if I wanted a Coke.

'No,' I said, 'I wouldn't have time to go to the restroom.'

It appeared the Expos had won the game in the 16th inning on a sacrifice fly. However, the Dodgers appealed that the base runner on third base had left before the catch was made.

Umpire Bob Davidson called the runner out while the Montreal players were celebrating. And the game went on and on and on.

The score was still 0–0 entering the 22nd inning. Montreal brought in starting pitcher Dennis Martinez to relieve. The Dodgers sent to the plate Rick Dempsey, who had caught Martinez when they were together in Baltimore. Dempsey had hit only one home run that season.

Against Martinez, Dempsey hit a low line drive that just cleared the left-field fence, and the Dodgers led 1–0.

In the bottom of the 22nd, Rex Hudler reached first base for the Expos. With two out, he attempted to steal second, and Dempsey threw him out to end the five-hour, 14-minute marathon.

Research afterward disclosed that no Major League Baseball announcer had ever broadcast a game by himself that lasted that long. It's nice to know that I am in the record book.

During our long flight home after the game, I heard on my radio that Pete Rose had been banned from baseball.

CHAPTER 5
THE 1990s

Ramon K's 18

There was one bright spot in a relatively lackluster 1990 season for the Dodgers. On June 4 the Dodgers took on the Atlanta Braves at Dodger Stadium, and Ramon Martinez put himself in the team record book alongside the immortal Sandy Koufax by striking out 18 Braves in a 6–0 victory.

Throwing a fastball that was clocked at 96 mph, Martinez tied the club record set twice by Koufax and was one short of the then-NL record of 19 shared by Steve Carlton and Tom Seaver.

"There were a couple of pitches where he let it go and—Boof!— the ball was in the catcher's glove. I never even saw it," Dodgers third baseman Mike Sharperson said.

Martinez ended the eighth with 18 strikeouts, giving him three shots at setting the record for the Dodgers and for all of baseball.

But it was not to be, as pinch-hitter Tommy Gregg popped to second, Oddibe McDowell grounded to first, and Jim Presley grounded to short. It was the only inning in which Martinez failed to get a strikeout.

"I was throwing as hard as I was in the beginning. I was doing everything I could do," Martinez said after the game. "I still got the complete game and the shutout, and we won. And I am with a super-star like Sandy Koufax. I feel honored."

Martinez struck out the side twice and struck out five consecutive batters twice.

Martinez's best season was 1990 as he finished 20–6 with a 2.92 ERA and 223 strikeouts in 234.1 innings. He finished second in Cy Young Award voting to Pittsburgh's Doug Drabek, who led the Pirates to the NL East title.

Fernandomania's Last Hurrah

Fernandomania was about two years past its shelf life in 1990. Valenzuela was a shadow of the pitcher he once was. After getting injured in 1988, he went 10–13 in 1989 and was off to a poor start in 1990. The fans still loved him, but he didn't draw sellouts for every start anymore and was just one of the guys—until June 29.

For one night, it seemed the spirit of the old Fernando inhabited the body of the broken-down Fernando as he tossed an unlikely no-hitter against the St. Louis Cardinals.

The day started with Oakland's Dave Stewart throwing a no-hitter against the Toronto Blue Jays. Valenzuela watched the final outs of the game on a TV in the clubhouse, turned to manager Tommy Lasorda and said, "That's great, now maybe we'll see another no-hitter."

Kreskin couldn't have been more proud.

The final outs came in the ninth with a runner on first, one out, and former teammate Pedro Guerrero at the plate. Guerrero hit a bouncer up the middle that ticked off Fernando's glove and rolled right to second baseman Juan Samuel, who stepped on second and threw to first for an inning-ending and no-hitter-preserving double play.

"Do you think if I don't touch that ball, it goes through for a single?" Valenzuela said after the game. "Whoa. I think it does. I think I don't touch it, I'm in trouble."

Valenzuela said he started to tire in the seventh inning.

"But this was a different kind of tired. This kind of tired did not bother me. You think I felt anything during that last inning? No way."

It was the last shining moment for Valenzuela, as 1990 would be his final season with the team.

"It couldn't have happened to a tougher, more competitive guy," Lasorda said. "You look at Fernando and he has done everything in his career except a no-hitter. And now this."

The only person not happy about the no-hitter was Guerrero.

"I'm not very happy right now. No way am I congratulating anybody. Maybe later, but not now."

The End of Fernandomania

Heading into the 1991 season, the Dodgers had a surplus of starting pitchers. Seven pitchers—Ramon Martinez, Tim Belcher, Mike Morgan, Bob Ojeda, Kevin Gross, Orel Hershiser, and Fernando Valenzuela—were battling for five rotation spots. It was obvious in spring training that Hershiser, coming off major shoulder surgery, wouldn't be ready to go, so that left one more pitcher on the bubble. But little thought was given to the fact it might be Fernando.

Valenzuela had a sub-par 1990, finishing 13–13 but with a 4.59 ERA, the worst of any regular NL starter that season. In spring training in 1991, he was considered safe to make the team, but then he struggled badly.

After a particularly poor start against Philadelphia, the Dodgers' brain trust of owner Peter O'Malley, general manager Fred Claire, and manager Tommy Lasorda knew that Valenzuela wasn't one of their best five starters and that he took too long to warm up, so he couldn't be a reliever.

There was only one thing left to do—release him.

"They called me into the office and said, 'This is very hard for us,'" Valenzuela said. "I said, 'What is so hard? Just say it!' And so they said it.

"I said, 'Okay, thanks.' And that is all I say.'"

In a 2013 interview, Claire remembered that day. "It was difficult to tell Fernando we were releasing him in spring training, but it was a move based on Fernando's performance that spring.

"I wanted to bring Fernando into spring training to give him every opportunity to win a spot in our starting rotation. As the spring games played out, it was clear Fernando wasn't going to be able to be one of our starting pitchers. We had a solid staff, and Fernando hadn't shown the performance to win a starting spot.

"It was difficult because Fernando had contributed so much and was such a warrior. I thought it was best that he had the chance as opposed to releasing him at the end of the previous season and not giving him the opportunity to stay with the Dodgers. I think if one looks back at how our staff performed that year, the results show it was the right move.

"That being said, it was difficult because Fernando was the ultimate warrior and had done so much for the Dodgers."

Fernando's teammates, make that ex-teammates, were stunned.

"It's one of those things that's tough to swallow. It's just very surprising," said catcher Mike Scioscia, who caught Fernando during the pitcher's entire Dodgers career. "There is no doubt he can still pitch and get guys out. I still have a lot of confidence in the guy. Some guys get in tough situations and they melt. This guy fights all the way to the end."

Reliever Tim Crews thought that someone was playing an early April Fools joke on him. "I said 'Man, I don't believe it.' I know things haven't been going too well for him, but with a competitor like him, he will win games for you. He will resurface somewhere, just watch."

And resurface he did, signing with the California Angels. Valenzuela bounced from team to team until 1997, when he retired.

Dodgers broadcaster Jaime Jarrin best summed up what Fernando meant to the Dodgers and to baseball. "He turned a game into a religion," Jarrin said. "Here was a hero who did not speak English, who did not have a good body, who came from a humble background but who walked like a general. All of a sudden, people who did not care about the game, because of Fernando they cared.

"You would come to the park on nights he would pitch, and there would be hundreds of people waiting outside, selling T-shirts and postcards with his picture on them. It was unbelievable."

The Straw

The Dodgers ended the 1990 season in second place with an 86–76 record. Heading into the off-season, the team wanted to add one more bat to complement first baseman Eddie Murray. The marquee free agent—Mets outfielder Darryl Strawberry, who grew up in the L.A. area and wanted to return home after several stormy seasons with the New York Mets where he had averaged better than 30 homers a season but had alienated many teammates with his headstrong personality.

On November 8, the Dodgers and Strawberry reached an agreement on a five-year, $20.25 million contract. The Dodgers were sure they had just bought a World Series title.

"I'd compare it to Bruce McNall's signing of Wayne Gretzky for the Kings," manager Tommy Lasorda said. "Darryl Strawberry is one of the outstanding players in baseball. I couldn't sleep after I heard the news."

Strawberry was equally ebullient. "I wanted to be with a winner, which the Dodgers have always been. I wanted to come home. I mean, people talk about the pressure of playing at home, but after going through what I went through in New York, nothing can be as bad as that.

"The pressure and expectations, the feeling the media created that every time the club failed it was because of me, took all the fun out of it. Now I feel that the fun is just beginning, that my career is just beginning. I think you'll see Darryl Strawberry take his game to new levels. There's no telling what I might produce. I've come here to help the Dodgers win a championship."

For one season, all seemed perfect. Strawberry hit .265 with 28 homers and 99 RBIs in his first season with the team, but the Dodgers finished one game behind the Atlanta Braves in the NL West.

Then it all fell apart.

Being back in his hometown did Strawberry no favors. He stayed out late with his old friends, fell out of shape, and injuries sidelined him for most of the next two seasons, during which he played in only 75 games.

Fred Claire, general manager of the Los Angeles Dodgers, holds a jersey with new Dodgers player Darryl Strawberry in Los Angeles, California, on Thursday, November 8, 1990. Strawberry signed a five-year, $20.25 million contract. Accompanying Strawberry are his wife, Lisa, two-year-old daughter, Diamond, and five-year-old son, Darryl Jr. *(AP Photo/Bob Galbraith)*

After a relatively quiet spring training in 1994, the Dodgers headed to the exhibition finale against the Angels relatively optimistic. There was one problem before the game started, however, Strawberry was nowhere to be found.

No one knew where he was. He had disappeared after Saturday night's exhibition game, and no one could locate him before Sunday's game.

Finally, late Sunday, Strawberry turned up. He told GM Fred Claire that he had overslept and then had car trouble. Claire wasn't buying it for a minute.

"I have spoken to Darryl, and he is with his family," Claire said in a prepared statement. "I am not satisfied with the explanation he has given me for his failure to report for the game today. I intend to meet with

Darryl again to review the matter in detail and to determine what the appropriate disciplinary action will be. This type of behavior is extremely detrimental to the ballclub and will not be tolerated."

On Monday, the two met again, and Strawberry came clean. He had been on a 24-hour cocaine binge.

So on the day of the Dodgers' season opener, the team announced that Strawberry would be entering himself into a substance-abuse program and would miss an undetermined part of the season.

"I'm just glad he's faced it," Claire said. "I guess it's just a difficult problem, and a big part of it obviously is denial. When you see Darryl playing well, performing well, in the clubhouse, on time, getting along with his teammates, good attitude, that's pretty tough to break all of that down and try to read something else into it."

Strawberry's attorney, Robert Shapiro, the same Robert Shapiro who would go on to be one of O.J. Simpson's defense attorneys during the former running back's murder trial, said Strawberry told him he was driven to drugs to try to relieve the pressure of playing in his home town.

"The stress of performing, the stress of coming back and performing at the level that a ballplayer of his reputation is expected to do," Shapiro said. "There are high expectations for him every time he steps up to the plate."

Strawberry, who had checked into the Betty Ford Clinic, completed treatment on May 4. But the Dodgers did not welcome him back with open arms, releasing him on May 25.

"I'm grateful to the Dodgers and the city of Los Angeles for the opportunity to have played in this great city," Strawberry said in a statement. "I regret that I did not live up to everyone's expectations, but I have received a lot of support during the period of rehabilitation and I will always be thankful for it."

Claire considers the entire chapter to be sad.

"I had great expectations when we signed Darryl," Claire said. "He was in the prime of his career, and all you had to do was look in the record books to see what he had accomplished. As far as his age, his coming back to the city of Los Angeles was a tremendous opportunity for the Dodgers.

"Our hopes and plans were that Darryl would keep us in contention while we developed our young outfield talent and be a key player for the team. He did a great deal for us in '91, and I still say his back injury led to his downfall in '92 and '93."

Strawberry signed with the San Francisco Giants in June then he moved on to the New York Yankees from 1995 to 1999, where he was a member of three World Series title teams.

A Really Gross Moment

If you look up "journeyman pitcher" in a dictionary, you will find a two-word definition: Kevin Gross. If you ran a major league team in the 1980s and '90s and wanted a solid No. 3 or No. 4 pitcher, a guy who would keep you in games and throw 200 innings a year, Kevin Gross was your man.

Gross pitched in the majors from 1983 to 1997, compiling a 142–158 record and a 4.11 ERA. Not the stuff of legend, which made the events of August 17, 1992, even more improbable.

The Dodgers were taking on the San Francisco Giants. Gross, who was off to a miserable start, came into the game with a 5–12 record. Nine innings later, he reached baseball immortality by pitching a no-hitter.

"It makes up for a not-so-good year for the Dodgers and myself," Gross said. "It brought tears to my eyes, no doubt about it."

Gross walked two and hit a batter, and it was the first time he had won a game in five weeks.

How unusual was the no-hitter? In Gross' 368 career starts, it was the only time he had given up fewer than three hits.

139

The Death of Don Drysdale

D odgers legend Don Drysdale died of a heart attack on July 3, 1993, while on the road with the team in Montreal. He was one of the team's broadcasters at the time, and his unexpected death hit the Dodgers hard.

"Don represented the Dodgers more than anybody who has ever worn the uniform," Ron Cey said moments after learning of Drysdale's death.

"I used to love it when he would talk baseball with me," Mickey Hatcher said. "He would talk about how they used to do it, how they used to feel, how they used to have fire.

"Don would talk about how you weren't supposed to love the other team, you were supposed to hate them. You know, there was a lot to what he said."

"If a young pitcher today had none of Drysdale's talent but all of his competitiveness, he'd win a lot of games," former Dodgers general manager Buzzie Bavasi said. "He was always Alston's favorite because Walter knew he'd be there every fourth day."

The day after Drysdale's death, former teammate Claude Osteen explained how Drysdale could carry and motivate a team.

"In 1966, we were four games out with 11 to play. Don got me and Ron Fairly alone one night and convinced us that the race could still be won. He then told us to go spread the word to the rest of the team.

"Many of us may not have really believed we had that kind of team, but we came back to steal it. Don carried a lot of credibility and weight. No disrespect to Sandy [Koufax], he certainly did his thing on the mound. But people saw Don as the one true Dodger. He was the spokesman for all of us."

After hearing the sad news, Orel Hershiser thought about breaking Drysdale's scoreless innings streak record in 1988. "He could have made it difficult for me, but he didn't. He kept his distance and didn't talk with me about it when it was going on. And after I broke the record in San Diego, he was there on the bench to greet me, and I will never forget what he said. He told me, 'At least we kept it in the family.'"

There is no finer tribute to Drysdale than that. He was a Dodger through and through.

Mike Piazza, Giant Slayer

The Dodgers finished the 1993 season with an 81–81 record, way behind the Atlanta Braves and San Francisco Giants, who battled it out all season for the NL West title.

The lone bright spot for the Dodgers in 1993 was the play of rookie catcher Mike Piazza, who was a unanimous Rookie of the Year winner after finishing the season with a .318 average to go along with 35 homers and 112 RBIs.

Any Dodgers fan will tell you that if it's clear the Dodgers won't win the division in a season, then the next-best thing is to make sure the Giants don't make the playoffs. Piazza, already becoming a fan favorite, captured the hearts of all Dodgers fans with his performance in the final game of the season.

The Dodgers played host to the Giants in that final game. San Francisco went into the game with a 103–58 record, but that was only good enough to tie the Braves. The Braves won their game early Sunday morning, so the Giants needed to defeat the Dodgers to force a one-game playoff with the Braves.

With his two best starters, 20-game winners Bill Swift and John Burkett, having pitched Thursday and Friday, Giants manager Dusty Baker faced a tough choice as to who to start that crucial Sunday game.

No other starter had more than eight wins for the Giants, but Baker made a surprising pick anyway—rookie Salomon Torres, who had made

Catcher Mike Piazza warms up before a spring training exhibition game in Vero Beach, Florida, on March 1, 1994. *(AP Photo/Mark Lennihan)*

only seven starts in his major league career. Giants fans were critical of the move, thinking the pressure was too much for a young pitcher.

They were right.

Before the game started, manager Tommy Lasorda gave his team an impassioned speech, reminding them of the times the Giants had broken the Dodgers' hearts. Bobby Thomson in 1951. The three-game playoff in 1962. Joe Morgan in 1982. It was time to exorcise those ghosts.

"We had a little meeting before the game, and Tommy gave us a little pep talk," outfielder Cory Snyder said. "Tommy came in and started reciting the stats and times that the Giants had knocked the Dodgers out of the pennant, and that seemed to be all the incentive we needed."

The fired-up Dodgers knocked out Torres in the fourth inning and had a 3–1 lead in the bottom of the fifth. That is when Piazza went to work.

Piazza hit a first-pitch fastball from Dave Burba deep into the right-field pavilion, a shot estimated at 365', the longest homer hit in Dodger Stadium that season. Cory Snyder hit a two-run homer later in the inning, and suddenly the Dodgers were up 6–1. The Dodgers tacked on a run in the bottom of the sixth and led 7–1.

But this Giants team featured Barry Bonds, who had 46 homers that year, so no lead was safe.

Piazza made sure the lead was safe.

In the bottom of the eighth, Piazza came up with two men on and launched a homer deep into the left-field pavilion. This was measured at 360', the second-longest homer hit at Dodger Stadium that season.

Not only that, Dodger fans, notorious (unfairly so) for having a blasé attitude, demanded a curtain call and gave Piazza a two-minute standing ovation.

The Dodgers won the game 12–1, embarrassing the Giants.

Piazza put his gear on to catch the top of the ninth when Lasorda sent out backup Carlos Hernandez to replace him. At first, Piazza didn't realize what was going on until he started to walk back to the dugout and saw the sellout crowd at Dodger Stadium on its feet, giving him another standing ovation.

"Then I knew what Tommy was doing," said Piazza, who received three curtain calls.

Nomomania

It went little-noticed in L.A. when it appeared as a small note in most papers on February 13, 1995. The Dodgers had signed a new pitcher, Hideo Nomo, who could possibly make the starting rotation. If he did, he would be only the second person to come from the Japanese major leagues to pitch in the U.S. major leagues.

Little did anyone realize that the small note would lead to the biggest phenomenon in L.A. since Fernandomania.

Unlike the buzz around Valenzuela, Nomomania was a slow build. After his first three starts, Nomo wasn't a big deal in L.A. He had a record of 0–0 with a 5.27 ERA. Two of his starts had been on the road, and this was before every game was televised, so many people hadn't seen him pitch at all.

His fourth start was at home against the Pittsburgh Pirates. Nomo struck out 14 in seven innings. The buzz began to build.

Two starts later, Nomo was on national TV for the first time. Fans got a good look at his unusual "tornado" delivery in which he would hold his arms high above his head, pivot to show his back to the catcher, then whirl around to throw the pitch.

On June 14, Nomo struck out 16 Pirates in an 8–5 victory. Suddenly he was 3–1 with a 2.84 ERA and 75 strikeouts in 57 innings.

Nomomania was born. Every home start after that was a sellout. In Japan, Nomo became a national hero.

Hideo Nomo pitches in the All-Star Game on July 11, 1995, in Arlington, Texas. *(AP Photo/Eric Gay)*

"It's gotten crazy around here. It's like the whole country knows everything about the Dodgers now," Hidemi Kittaka, who lived in Japan at the time, said. "Everybody talks about Mike Piazza and his power. They don't like Jose Offerman because he keeps making errors in Nomo's games. Men like me are so proud of Nomo and what he's doing for our country. And you talk to women now, and they say, 'Oh, I didn't know Nomo was so cute.'"

Nomo hated the attention. "Sometimes I wish I was just another player. My privacy is very limited. I feel so restricted."

Nomo was great for the economy, too, as many Japanese tourists came to L.A. in hopes of seeing him pitch. "It's a long way to travel and a lot of money to pay," Japan Travel Bureau agent Michitaka Kawashima told the Associated Press in 1995. "Not even knowing for sure that he'll pitch at the game they've come to see. But Nomo is such a big hit that lots of people are willing to take the risk."

Nomomania reached its apogee on September 17, 1996, when he pitched a no-hitter against the Colorado Rockies in Denver's Coors Field, a park known for high scores because of its mile-high altitude.

"Throwing a no-hitter at this place," his catcher for the game, Mike Piazza, said, "he should be canonized on the spot."

Manager Bill Russell compared him to another mania. "To me, he's like Fernando. Those guys say, 'Give me the ball.' He's a big-game guy. Nothing seems to bother him. He's had to overcome the language and cultural barriers, and here he is with a no-hitter. That's a special person to do what he's doing."

Nomomania burned bright but briefly. He was traded to the New York Mets after getting off to a horrible start in 1998, but Dodgers fans never forgot him and gave him a warm ovation on Hideo Nomo bobblehead doll night at Dodger Stadium in 2013.

Tommy Steps Down

In 1996, Tommy Lasorda had been the Dodgers manager for 20 seasons, and seemed like a walking advertisement for the unstoppable force. He had managed the team to two World Series titles, four National League pennants, and seven division titles. He was a walking monument to bleeding Dodger blue and had the heart of a lion.

Then that heart betrayed him.

Lasorda, then 68, went to the hospital in late June because of stomach pains, which was no surprise to anyone who had seen him eat. It seemed as if every postgame news conference took place in Lasorda's office while he was eating a mound of spaghetti.

Doctors checked him out and said his stomach ache was actually a heart attack. Doctors performed angioplasty to open an artery that was 75 percent blocked.

"He's very fortunate," said cardiologist Anthony Reid, who performed the surgery at Centinela Hospital Medical Center. "It could've been a very serious problem. We caught it in the nick of time, so to speak. It was a minor heart attack."

Of course, a minor heart attack is any heart attack that happens to anyone else but you.

The Dodgers quickly said Lasorda's job was still open for him, and it was assumed he would be back in a couple of weeks. Meanwhile, Bill Russell took over as interim manager and led the team as speculation began to build as to *when* Lasorda would return. After a couple of weeks, speculation began to change to *if* Lasorda would return.

Finally, in late July, Lasorda called *Los Angeles Times* columnist Allan Malamud and said that he was going to retire and become a vice president of the organization. When asked why he was stepping down, Lasorda said it was too much for his weakened heart.

"For me to get into a uniform again—as excitable as I am—I could not go down there without being the way I am," Lasorda said. "I decided it's best for me and the organization to step down.... That's quite a decision."

Reaction was immediate, and not just from players.

"Tommy is the heart and soul of the Dodgers," Frank Sinatra said. "His loyalty to the organization knows no bounds. And now that he has some time, Tommy can brush up on his singing—I'm always looking for a good opening act."

Comedian Don Rickles even put away the insults for a moment to say, "Tommy was a great motivator. Whenever I went to a game and I said to him, 'I've got a headache,' he made it seem like in 20 minutes I'd be dancing at a wedding. He made everything positive, which I love and respect him for that to this day."

Ron Cey looked back at Lasorda's career, particularly the way he treated young players. "For us to be growing up with a guy who didn't have a clock that was punched 9 to 5 was great. The day wasn't over with in spring training when it was 4:00 in the afternoon—if we wanted to do more, we did more, and sometimes we did it until it got dark.

"He basically surrounded himself with the nucleus of the team while they were in the minor leagues that became the Dodgers of the '70s and early '80s. It was a great honor for us to have a guy like that who was in our corner and worked as hard as he did."

Atlanta manager Bobby Cox, a longtime friend of Lasorda, said he was surprised at the news but knew of a good spot for him. "Knowing Tommy, I thought he was coming back for sure. He's one of those guys we can't afford to let go out of baseball, and I'm glad the Dodgers are making him a vice president. He's still going to be connected with the Dodgers, but his blood pressure will be a lot lower. I always thought he was baseball's best ambassador ever. If you mention baseball, you think of Tommy. We better be ashamed of ourselves if he doesn't go into the Hall of Fame on the first ballot."

Lasorda was elected to the Hall of Fame by the Veterans Committee on the first ballot in 1997, the same year the Dodgers retired his No. 2. But Lasorda did not go meekly into the night.

Four years after he retired, Lasorda managed the U.S. to an unlikely gold medal at the 2000 Summer Olympics in Sydney. He remained a fixture at most Dodgers home games for many years, basking in the love from the fans as he sat in his seat near the Dodgers' dugout. In many ways, it was like he never left (though the Dodgers certainly had trouble filling his managerial shoes).

Tommy Lasorda passed away on January 7, 2021, at the age of 93.

Trading Mike Piazza

In 1998, Mike Piazza, the greatest hitting catcher of all time, was in the final year of his contract. Negotiations between the Dodgers and Piazza on a multiyear deal dragged on through spring training that year with the two sides far apart on terms. Piazza wanted a seven-year, $100 million deal. The Dodgers were looking more along the lines of six years, $75 million. However, it seemed unthinkable that the Dodgers would let their franchise player leave, so most Dodgers fans felt relatively confident that a deal would eventually be reached.

To the surprise of many, Piazza chose to blast the Dodgers on Opening Day. "I'm not going to lie and say I'm not concerned about this, that I'm not confused and disappointed by the whole thing—because I am. I'm mad that this has dragged into the season, and that it now has the potential to become a distraction. I'm not going to use this as an excuse if things aren't going well because that wouldn't be fair to the fans or my teammates. But how can I not think about this?

"If they say they have the intent to sign me, then sign me. But if they don't have the intent to sign me, then just let me know so at least I'll be able to start to think about having a future somewhere else after the season. But what they're doing now, the way this is going, I just don't get it."

If Piazza's intention was to garner sympathy from the fans as a negotiating ploy, it backfired badly. Dodgers fans took umbrage with his veiled comment that the negotiations might affect his play on the field. When the Dodgers played their first home game of the season, Piazza was lustily booed when he was announced. He was booed when he walked to the plate. He was booed when he walked back to the dugout.

"You don't like it," Piazza said about the boos. "But I was just trying to concentrate on my job. I've got a lot of responsibilities out there. That's all there is to it. Everything else has to stay in the background. If fans are upset a little bit, that's fine. I'm sorry for that. But I'm not the first guy in baseball to be booed and probably not the last."

One thing throwing a monkey wrench into the negotiations was the fact that the team was changing owners. Longtime owner Peter O'Malley was selling the Dodgers to Rupert Murdoch and the Fox Group, and the Piazza contract discussions were taking place while the executives at Fox were going over all of the Dodgers' financial statements. Would the Dodgers even be able to add a huge salary while all this was going on? And if so, who had final approval, O'Malley or Murdoch? New Dodgers president Bob Graziano was doing a lot of talking to the media about the deal, but what about GM Fred Claire? What was his role?

All these questions lingered until May 14 when the unthinkable happened—the Dodgers traded Piazza and third baseman Todd Zeile to the Florida Marlins for outfielder Gary Sheffield, third baseman Bobby Bonilla, outfielder Jim Eisenreich, catcher Charles Johnson, and pitcher Manuel Barrios.

The most unhappy man in L.A. that day may have been Fred Claire, who was supposed to be the man in charge of decisions like this.

Graziano thought otherwise, as he made the deal behind Claire's back without even consulting him for his opinion.

"I recommended the deal to people at Fox," Graziano said. "I think this helps improve our chemistry, helps improve our hitting, and helps improve our defense. I think the team is markedly improved."

Meanwhile, reaction from Dodgers fans, who had still been booing Piazza since his opening-day comments, was along the lines of, "Hey, we didn't mean it. Why in the world would you trade him?" Suddenly, Dodgers fans were bemoaning the fact the team didn't give him the seven years and $100 million he was asking for.

"He's worth every penny," Mark Curtis said. "I was just afraid San Francisco was going to pay him."

"We love Mike Piazza. We want him here," James Thomas said. "He brings a lot of money to the organization. He brings a lot of fans. They keep trading away the good guys, trading them and losing them to free agency. Mike Piazza is okay. He brings out the best in fans at a game, gives them a good feeling, and makes them want to come to a baseball game. I like him, and it just baffles me that he's not going to be a Dodger."

George Anderson blamed the Dodgers' new owners. "It's the almighty dollar. This wouldn't have happened if the O'Malleys still owned the club. They were like family."

It was the end of an era for the team. To this day, some fans say that was the day they stopped being Dodgers fans.

During his seven-year Dodgers career, Piazza hit .331 with 177 homers and 563 RBIs. He spent one week with the Marlins before they traded him to the New York Mets for prospects. In 2016, Piazza was elected to the Hall of Fame and went in as a Met.

Claire's book, *My 30 Years in Dodger Blue*, was an invaluable resource for this section and other parts of this book. In it, Claire looked back on the trade in a 2013 interview.

"I felt it was a terrible trade for the Dodgers on two major counts—the Dodgers lost a franchise player and future Hall of Fame player in Mike; and the team took on a significant salary in Bobby Bonilla [$5.9 million a year for three seasons], and he was a player who I didn't feel could help the Dodgers.

"It seemed as though every time Bobby was a free agent, I would receive a call from his agent, but each time I stated we didn't have an interest. And now here he was a Dodger."

Claire said he had no intention of trading Piazza, especially since it was only May, more than two months before the trade deadline. "I never made a call to a team stating that we had an interest in trading Mike. I never wanted those discussions to begin because the last thing I wanted to do was to trade Mike. The only time Mike's name came up in a trade discussion was when I received a call from Marlin GM Dave Dombrowski after the start of the 1998 season. Dave wanted to know if I would consider trading Piazza for outfielder Gary Sheffield, catcher Charles Johnson, outfielder Jim Eisenreich, and a young pitcher.

"I told Dave I had no interest in trading Mike, but I would have an interest in Sheffield. If we added Sheffield to a lineup that included Piazza, Eric Karros, Raul Mondesi, and Todd Zeile, we would have one of the strongest lineups in the National League."

Dodgers history would have been very different if the new owners had left everything alone and let Claire do the job he was hired to do.

"I believe that we would have been able to sign Mike if the trade hadn't been made because I felt Mike wanted to remain a Dodger. We realized it was going to be a difficult negotiation, but that comes with the territory of signing a superstar player. After all, the Dodgers signed pitcher Kevin Brown as a free agent after the season for an enormous contract.

"The most shocking thing about the trade was that it was made in May, not July when the trading deadline rolled around. Furthermore, if the new owners [and] Fox really wanted to get value for Mike in a trade, it would have made sense to explore discussions with a number of teams."

Imagine the Dodgers with Mike Piazza after 1998. Would they have made the playoffs more often? Would they have won a World Series or two? Impossible to say, but Dodgers fans would have had a lot of fun finding out.

Cleaning House

Fox wasn't done making big moves, however. Six weeks after trading Piazza, with the team a disappointing 36–38, the team fired manager Bill Russell and general manager Fred Claire. All this coming from an organization that had employed only two managers from 1954 to 1996 and only two GMs from 1968 until the day Claire was fired.

Perhaps learning a lesson from the nightmarish reaction from fans to the Piazza trade, team president Bob Graziano invited former owner Peter O'Malley to the news conference and namedropped him often.

"Peter O'Malley and I met with Fred and Bill earlier this evening and informed them that we were making a change," Graziano said. "I spent a great deal of time over the past few days thinking about this and discussing it with Peter, and I felt a change needed to be made in order for the team to improve and get back on track.

"I mostly consulted with Peter O'Malley. Peter spent many years in the organization and many years with the people that this decision will impact."

O'Malley, who still commanded the respect and loyalty of Dodgers fans even though he had no real role with the team anymore, said he was in favor of the moves.

"The team was flat, the intensity was missing," O'Malley said. "I told Fred that the team appeared to be flat as far back as spring training. He said there were injuries, that some players weren't ready yet for the season, but we were a .500 team in April and May and now it's the latter part of June. It's disappointing. We're spending an incredible amount of money on scouting, player development, and major league payroll. There aren't too many organizations, if any, that exceed what we're paying in those areas and, quite simply, it wasn't working. The team wasn't responding.

"Would it have been better to wait until the end of the season to make these moves? I don't think so. Based on the team's performance, there was a doubt in my mind and Bob's mind that Fred and Bill would be back next year, and therefore this gives us more time to prepare and plan. It gives Bob and Tommy time to search out the best general manager they can find without having to wait until the fall."

O'Malley's words seemed to soothe Dodgers fans who reacted to the firings of Russell and Claire with relative indifference when compared to the Piazza trade.

Russell had been with the Dodgers for 32 years as a player, coach, and manager. He became the first Dodgers manager to be fired since Charlie Dressen was fired after the 1953 season. Claire was in his 30th year with the Dodgers.

To replace the two, the Dodgers named Glenn Hoffman manager and named former manager Tommy Lasorda as the new GM.

"I was with the organization for 32 years, and you just don't forget that," Russell said. "Being fired is part of the game—and the reality of seeing it happen to other people, I knew it could happen to me."

Russell and Claire combined to give more than 60 years of service to the team, and they have only been back to Dodger Stadium a few times since they were fired.

"I have been back to Dodger Stadium a few times but to only a couple of games," Claire said. "After Fox sold the team, Maury Wills invited me to attend Opening Day in 2013 with him, and he is a friend who I never would turn down.

"I've been to the stadium a few times to do television interviews or to visit with friends in the Dodger organization. Very frankly, I enjoy the visits when the stadium is empty or if there are players on the field for early workouts before the crowd gathers.

"I loved every day I walked into Dodger Stadium, and that feeling still holds true and always will. It's a special place, and a lot of my heart is there.

"I think the new Dodger owners have been great, and they are very gracious. I saw Magic at an event at the Rose Bowl one day and he said, 'Fred, we just want to accomplish the things that you fellows accomplished.'

"Those words mean a lot."

CHAPTER 6

THE 2000s

Eric the Forgotten

The Dodgers have had many great power hitters during their long history in Los Angeles: Steve Garvey, Ron Cey, Reggie Smith, Rick Monday, Mike Piazza, Gary Sheffield, Shawn Green, and Matt Kemp. But who is the greatest of them all?

Eric Karros.

Not many fans would guess Eric Karros if you asked them who has hit the most home runs for the L.A. Dodgers, but he finished his career with the team with 270 home runs, far outdistancing Cey, who is in second with 228. Karros is the forgotten man in Dodgers history. Ask people to name the 10 greatest Dodgers off all time and he probably won't be listed, but he is in the top 10 in almost every offensive category.

Part of the problem is that he played during one of the worst eras as far as Dodgers success is concerned. Karros was with the team from 1991 to 2002, a period during which the team only made the playoffs twice and was swept out of the postseason both times, not winning a single game.

Karros broke Cey's home run record on June 13, 2000, when his drive against Arizona's Matt Mantei just cleared the left-field fence in the eighth inning of a 6–1 victory.

Of course, it's easy to understand why Karros gets overlooked nowadays when you look at his understated reaction to setting the record.

"This was just a side note to the game. It's nice to be mentioned along with guys like Ron Cey and Steve Garvey," Karros said. "But I'd rather be mentioned with them in world championships."

What was that guy's name again? Eric who?

Gang Green

Needing some power in the lineup, the Dodgers acquired Shawn Green from the Toronto Blue Jays for outfielder Raul Mondesi before the 2000 season. Green hit .309 with 42 homers for Toronto in 1999, so he was counted on to be the centerpiece of the offense.

The pressure of being the key man on the team was too much for Green, who admitted he was pressing and had a disappointing season, hitting only .269 with 24 home runs. He rebounded in 2001, hitting 49 home runs, but he saved his best work for one particular day during the 2002 season.

Going into the game on May 23, Green was off to his usual slow start, hitting just .238 with five homers. Then he put on the greatest offensive display in major league history.

The Dodgers were playing the Brewers in Milwaukee. Glendon Rusch got the start for the Brewers but didn't last long. He gave up a run-scoring double to Green in a three-run Dodgers first inning.

In the second inning, Green homered, driving in three runs. By the end of the inning, the Dodgers had an 8–0 lead and Rusch was done for the day. Green already had a double and a homer.

Green led off the fourth inning against Brian Mallette and lined a 1–1 pitch over the right-center fence for his second home run of the game.

In the fifth, Green knocked a 1–0 pitch over the fence in right. Suddenly, in only the fifth inning he had three home runs and a double and was guaranteed at least one more at-bat.

Green came up in the eighth with a chance at his fourth home run of the game. By this time, the Dodgers led 10–2, so even the Brewers fans were cheering for him, hoping to witness baseball history. Green got a fastball from Jose Cabrera but could "only" manage a single.

That appeared to be it. The Dodgers would have to string together some hits for Green to have another at-bat. After Green's single, Dave Hansen popped out, Hiram Bocachica homered (making it 12–2 Dodgers), Marquis Grissom grounded out, and Alex Cora flew out.

Strangely enough, though their team was getting routed, most of the Brewers faithful stayed for the ninth inning, hoping Green would get one more shot.

It didn't look good, though. Chad Kreuter began the ninth with a double, but Jeff Williams struck out and Jeff Reboulet popped to first. With two out, Adrian Beltre would have to reach base for Green to have another chance.

Beltre homered. It was probably the first time Brewers fans had ever cheered an opponent for hitting a home run. Green had one more chance.

Cabrera was still on the mound for the Brewers. He ran the count to 1–1 when he hung a breaking ball. Green launched it out of the park. Cheers rained down as he circled the bases—four home runs in one game, becoming only the 14th player in major league history to do so. He had five extra-base hits, tying a major league record. And he accumulated a major league record 19 total bases.

After the game, Green was in shock.

"It definitely hasn't sunk in yet. I wish I had a couple of days off so I could enjoy it. It's something I'll never forget. No one in this game needed this more than I did because I was getting pretty down. The ball had been looking like a ping-pong ball. Today it looked like a beach ball. It slowed down a lot. The last six weeks, the ball seemed to be going so fast I had a tough time, jumping at pitches. Today I was able to sit back and wait for it."

When he was with the Dodgers, Green had a tradition of handing out his batting gloves to a kid in the stands after each home run. It endeared him to the fans, who grew to appreciate their quiet, mild-mannered slugger. Hitting four home runs in a game didn't change him.

"He didn't showboat or anything," Brewers first-base coach Cecil Cooper said about Green's fourth homer. "He hit that last one, dropped his head, and that was it. He's a class kid."

Game Over

From 2002 to 2004, Eric Gagne did something that few players have been able to do—he made Dodgers fans pay close attention to the game.

During that time period, Gagne was the best closer in the game. Fans hoped the Dodgers would be leading by only a run or two going into the ninth inning of home games so they could see Gagne pitch. I was actually at games where fans booed whenever the Dodgers took a big lead because a big lead meant no Gagne. The Guns 'n Roses song "Welcome to the Jungle," which Gagne entered the game to, sent fans into rapturous joy. Gagne wore goggles, so fans started wearing goggles. "Game Over" T-shirts featuring Gagne's face on a blue background sold out and could be seen all over the city.

With his devastating fastball, Gagne saved an amazing 84 consecutive games during those years, a record unmatched in baseball history.

So it came as quite a shock on July 5, 2004, when Gagne was called upon to preserve a 5–3 lead over the Arizona Diamondbacks at Dodger Stadium and failed to do so. Streak over.

After striking out Scott Hairston to start the ninth inning, Gagne gave up a single to Shea Hillenbrand.

"I just tried to throw a curveball and it didn't come down, it just stayed up in the zone," Gagne said after the game. "I've been throwing that for a first-pitch strike, and I thought I was going to throw the same one, but he stayed back real well."

Gagne then gave up a run-scoring double to Luis Gonzalez, followed by a single to Chad Tracy that scored Gonzalez to tie the game. No save for Gagne. When the tying run scored, the fans gave Gagne a standing ovation. Gagne got the last two outs, and when he returned to the dugout, fans called him out for a curtain call. (By the way, the Dodgers won the game in extra innings.)

Closer Eric Gagne celebrates after he struck out Arizona Diamondback Steve Finley to end the game on Sunday, May 30, 2004, in Los Angeles. Gagne extended his major league–record saves streak to 75 with his 12th of the season. The Dodgers won 3–0. *(AP Photo/Mark J. Terrill)*

"I had fun," Gagne said when looking back at the streak. "Everybody says you have to be real lucky. I was real lucky for a long time. It just came to an end."

In the immediate aftermath of the game, his teammates paid tribute to Gagne.

"What he accomplished is unbelievable," Shawn Green said. "It's one of those records that will be with all the other huge records of baseball. Eighty-four consecutive saves will be a number people will remember. It's something that wasn't going to last forever, but it seemed like it would with the way he pitches."

Jim Tracy, who was managing the team at the time, said he didn't know how to react when the streak ended. "We just gave him a huge hug. You know something special has been taking place over the course of almost two seasons now when there's a blown save and our fans ask for a curtain call after a blown save. How many times have you ever seen that happen?"

True, some of the luster came off the streak when Gagne was named in the Mitchell Report as a performance-enhancing-drug user, but the memories will always remain.

In a lengthy 2010 interview, Gagne talked about the Mitchell Report and how it affected his view of the streak. "It changed it a lot for a couple of years," Gagne said. "But now you come to grips, where you know what, it is what it is. You have to accept it and just go on. You have to keep going and enjoy baseball, get people out and get back to basics. There are a lot of regrets. But the whole time I was with the Dodgers, it was an unbelievable time. The Mitchell Report and everything is negative. It's always going to be on my resume for the rest of my life."

Grand Finish

The 1990s turned out to be a lost decade, but the Dodgers started to turn things around in the new century. They started improving, little by little, each year. In 2002, they won 92 games, finishing third. They won 85 games in 2003 but moved up to second place, missing a playoff spot by three games. By 2004, they were challenging for the NL West title.

Going into the final weekend of the season, the Dodgers were three games ahead of the San Francisco Giants with three games to play. And wouldn't you know it? Those last three games would be against the Giants at Dodger Stadium—one win and the division was theirs.

The Dodgers lost the first game 4–2, thanks in part to a J.T. Snow home run. The loss made Dodgers fans a little nervous. It had been almost 10 years since the team last made the playoffs. They wouldn't blow it all in the season's last weekend, would they?

The second game of the series looked like more of the same. Giants center fielder Marquis Grissom knocked in three runs (two on a home run) as the Giants took a 3–0 lead heading into the bottom of the ninth with closer Dustin Hermanson on the mound. But the Dodgers weren't done yet.

Shawn Green led off the ninth with a single and moved to second when Robin Ventura walked. Alex Cora struck out, but pinch-hitter Jose Hernandez walked, loading the bases with one out. Hermanson, who couldn't find the strike zone with a GPS that day, walked pinch-hitter Hee-Seop Choi to force in a run, making it 3–1 Giants. That was enough for Giants manager Felipe Alou. He removed Hermanson and brought in Jason Christiansen. Cesar Izturis was at the plate. And then the game appeared to be over. Izturis hit a grounder to short, an easy double-play ball. Except shortstop Cody Ransom, brought into the game just that inning for his solid defense, kicked the ball. Ventura scored, and everybody else was safe. Bases still loaded, one out, and the Dodgers were trailing 3–2. That was all for Christiansen, as Alou made the lonely walk to the mound again to bring in former Dodger Matt Herges.

Up to the plate stepped Jayson Werth, who usually didn't play against right-handers. He worked the count to 2–2 and singled to right, scoring Hernandez with the tying run. The bases were still loaded, and Dodger Stadium was rocking.

That brought up Steve Finley, which brought out Alou again to bring in lefty Wayne Franklin to face the left-handed hitter.

The Dodgers acquired Finley at the trade deadline that season for three players who didn't amount to much (Reggie Abercrombie, Koyie Hill, and Bill Murphy). The worst part of coming over to a playoff-contending team at the deadline is that you never know how to really fit in. The team had been successful without you, so you don't want to damage the delicate chemistry formed by 25 players, but you want to feel like a full member of the squad.

It's safe to say that Finley felt like a full member after his at-bat against Franklin.

On Franklin's second pitch, Finley lifted a fly ball to right-center that cleared the fence and went about 15 rows up into the stands. In one of the more iconic Dodger images, Finley dropped his bat and threw his hands in the air the moment he hit the ball. The final score was Dodgers 7, Giants 3, and the Dodgers won the West. As the icing on the cake, the win also prevented the Giants from making the playoffs as a wild-card team, finishing one game behind the Houston Astros.

Why did Finley react at home plate the way he did?

"I wanted to enjoy the atmosphere," Finley said. "I knew it was out. I pictured myself getting the game-winning hit off Dustin Hermanson, but it wasn't him when I came to the plate. But still I knew I was going to get it done."

How incredible was the moment? John Shelby, the center fielder for the 1988 Dodgers, the last Dodgers team before 2020 to win the World

Series, summed it up. "I thought I'd never see it like 1988 again. But this is unbelievable. I can never remember dramatics like this."

Lima Time

The Dodgers faced the St. Louis Cardinals in the first round of the 2004 playoffs, searching for their first postseason victory since Game 5 of the 1988 World Series. And after two games, they were still searching. There was only one choice to make—Lima Time.

Jose Lima was a journeyman pitcher looking for a job before the 2004 season began. He went 21–10 and made the All-Star team with the 1999 Houston Astros, but struggled badly after that, going 7–16, 6–12, 5–10, 4–6, and 8–3 in the ensuing years.

He played for the Kansas City Royals in 2003, but they didn't want him back, figuring his 8–3 record was a fluke since he had a lofty 4.91 ERA.

But with no true staff ace, the Dodgers needed starting pitching. Hideo Nomo was fading badly, and the other three starters, Jeff Weaver, Odalis Perez, and Kaz Ishii, were stopgaps at best.

So they took a chance and signed Lima, figuring he could be their No. 5 starter. By the end of a 13–5, 4.07 ERA season, he was the team's No. 1 starter.

But it wasn't just solid pitching Lima brought to the team, he infused the team with life and enthusiasm. He would smooth the mound when he pitched and point excitedly at teammates when they made a great defensive play. He would slap his glove when he struck someone out and charge off the mound and into the dugout when the last out of an inning was made.

The fans loved him. Opponents hated him.

"Playing with him you come to realize that the energy you see on the mound isn't a false persona, that's Jose Lima," said Jim Tracy, who managed Lima when he played for the Dodgers. "He acts like that all the time, he's always happy-go-lucky, jumping around, joking, laughing. So that's who he is. There's nothing fake about him in that sense.

"There are times when opposing teams or players would get upset with the way he carries himself, but that was his energy. Even on days he wasn't pitching, he was like that. If it's honest emotion, I don't think anybody would really have a problem with it. But you have to get to know him to know that's how he is."

So the Dodgers, looking for their first playoff win in 16 years, sent Lima to the mound in Game 3 and hoped some of that enthusiasm would rub off on to a victory.

He responded with a five-hit shutout, his first complete game and first shutout of the season. Fans were with him from the first pitch on, pumping their fists and waving their rally towels.

"If there's such a thing as fans rising to another level," Tracy said, "then they did that that night."

The Cardinals never seriously threatened in the Dodgers' 4–0 victory, only getting two runners as far as second base. When Lima got Jim Edmonds on a pop fly to third to end the game, he dropped to one knee, said a prayer, and pumped his fist.

"I told you I was going to bring my 'A' game. I wasn't going to let these guys down," Lima said after the game. "I was going to bring every-thing I have in my heart for this ballclub and to the fans. Our season was not going to end this night. No way."

The 2004 season was Lima's only year with the Dodgers. He was looking for big money after his season, and Dodgers management didn't want to give it to him, feeling he probably pitched over his head that season.

They were right. Lima signed a one-year, $2.5 million deal with the Kansas City Royals in the off-season and finished with a 5–16 record with a 6.99 ERA. After going 0–4 with a 9.87 ERA the following year with the Mets, Lima retired.

Jose Lima died on May 23, 2010. Just two days before, he attended a game at Dodger Stadium. When he was shown sitting in the stands on the Dodgers DiamondVision videoboard in left field, the fans all rose to give him one more standing ovation. It was one last glimpse of Lima Time before time ran out.

Four-Gone Conclusion

It is the second-greatest regular-season game in Dodger Stadium history. (See the section of this book on the 1980s for the greatest.)

As the 2006 season neared its end, the Dodgers and San Diego Padres were neck-and-neck for the NL West lead. The night of September 18, 2006, they were facing each other with the Padres clinging to a half-game lead in the division. Whoever won would be in first place with about 12 games to go in the season.

The Padres scored four runs in the first, thanks in part to a booming double by former Dodger Mike Piazza.

The Dodgers responded with a run in the first, a run in the second, and two in the third to tie the score. By the time the eighth inning rolled around, it was tied at 4–4. The Padres scored twice to take a 6–4 lead, and again in the ninth when they scored three more runs to increase their lead to 9–5.

So things looked hopeless when the bottom of the ninth began. The Padres had Jon Adkins on the mound, but if the Dodgers even hinted at threatening, San Diego could always bring in Trevor Hoffman, one of the best closers in the game.

The Dodger Stadium crowd started to empty out when Jeff Kent led off the inning with the homer. "I was trying to get my mind ready for Hoffman," Kent said. "I was surprised he didn't come in after my hit."

The Dodgers celebrate as Nomar Garciaparra (5) touches home plate after hitting a walk-off two-run home run to defeat the San Diego Padres 11–10 in the 10th inning on Monday, September 18, 2006, in Los Angeles. *(AP Photo/Jeff Lewis)*

The homer was nice, but it was still 9–6. The next batter, J.D. Drew, also homered, making it 9–7. "We were still down three runs when I came up, so I was just trying to put a good swing on it," Drew said. "It went out of the park, so I guess I put a good swing on it."

Suddenly, some of those fans who were leaving rushed back to their seats.

Padres manager Bruce Bochy made the call everyone was expecting, bringing in Hoffman, and some of those same fans started heading back to the exits. No way the Dodgers would score two more runs. Not off Hoffman.

Russell Martin hit Hoffman's first pitch over the left-field fence, and the lead was reduced to 9–8 Padres. "The other day, he threw me a fastball, first pitch, belt-high. I didn't hit it. I was hoping I would get to see that pitch again," Martin said. "He threw me pretty much the same pitch. I didn't miss it."

What? Three straight homers? The Stadium seemed full again as the fans came to life. The Dodgers just needed one more run. A couple of hits would have done the trick because, surely, it was impossible for a team to hit four straight home runs.

Up to the plate stepped Marlon Anderson. Acquired at the August 31 trade deadline, Anderson had already homered once in the game. The odds of a player homering twice in one game, and that homer being the fourth consecutive his team had hit in the bottom of the ninth must have been about a gajillion to one. (Gajillion is a technical term, don't look it up).

Anderson swung at the first pitch. Bang. Home run. Amazing! Four straight homers to tie the score at 9–9. "What are the chances?" Anderson asked. "Four in a row in a baseball game? It's definitely the greatest game I've ever played in."

Well, it was the fourth time it had happened in major league history. Four times in about 200,000 games.

Hoffman retired the next three batters (for the record, Julio Lugo was the man who had the chance to make it five in a row), sending the game into extra innings. No one was leaving the stadium now.

The Dodgers brought in Aaron Sele to pitch the 10th, and he gave up a double, a walk, and a single to put the Padres ahead again 10–9 going into the bottom of the inning.

Well, four in a row was nice, but it doesn't mean much if you don't win the game.

Former Dodger Rudy Seanez pitched the 10th inning for the Padres. He walked Kenny Lofton and then faced Nomar Garciaparra. Bang. Home run. The Dodgers won 11–10 and moved into first place.

"When I was rounding the bases, I couldn't wait to get home and hug everybody," Garciaparra said. "It was like a group hug because it was a group effort."

The crowd was electric—no one wanted to leave—and the stadium remained packed 20 minutes after the game was over. The ushers had to plead with people to go home.

Even Vin Scully, who had seen everything, was stunned. "I walk outside 10 minutes after the game, and it seemed like every single driver of every single car was blowing their horn. It sounded like V-J Day."

It happened three times before that day (thanks to retrosheet.org for the information).

On June 8, 1961, with a 10–2 lead in the seventh, Cincinnati's Jim Maloney gave up home runs to Eddie Mathews and Hank Aaron. Marshall Bridges relieved Maloney and gave up home runs to Joe Adcock and Frank Thomas on his first two pitches. The Reds held on for a 10–8 victory.

On July 31, 1963, Angels pitcher Paul Foytack gave up consecutive home runs to Woodie Held, Pedro Ramos, Tito Francona, and Larry Brown, all on 0–2 counts.

And on May 2, 1964, Tony Oliva led off the 11th inning against the Kansas City A's Dan Pfister with a home run, and Bob Allison and Jimmie Hall followed suit—all on the first pitch. Vern Handrahan relieved Pfister and Harmon Killebrew hit his first pitch out.

Of course, most people only got to see the game one way—on TV. Luckily, they had the incomparable Scully calling the action.

Here are excerpts of his play-by-play during the ninth and 10th innings. The first starts in the ninth inning after home runs by Jeff Kent and J.D. Drew.

What is that line? 'Do not go gentle into that good night.' Well, the Dodgers have decided they are not gonna go into that good night without howling and kicking, and Bruce Bochy's going out to the mound to find out what's going on. So Jon Adkins is banished in a hurry, home runs by Kent and

Drew, but of course the Padres still have a two-run lead, and all of a sudden, it is Trevor time.

He has been absolutely magnificent against everybody, but especially the Dodgers. He is 55-for-57 in his career. He has saved 24 straight, and the last time Trevor Hoffman had a blown save against the Dodgers was in April five years ago.

And a drive into left-center by Martin, that ball is carrying…into the seats! Three straight home runs!

High and out. For Trevor Hoffman, he had allowed only two home runs. Russell Martin's dad is ecstatic [as a camera shows Martin's father dancing in the stands], the Dodgers are still a buck short on home runs by Kent and Drew and Martin. And now Marlon Anderson and Julio Lugo and the pitcher's spot. And the folks who hung around to ride it out are in for quite a ride. For the Dodgers, five home runs in the game tonight. First time they've done that this year.

And another drive into high right-center, at the wall, running and watching it go out, believe it or not! Four consecutive home runs! The Dodgers have tied it up again!

Scully paused as the crowd roared.

They're coming back in. The people in the parking lot have decided they'd better come back. And for Marlon Anderson, what a night! Two singles, a triple, and two home runs, a five-hit game, and we're 9–9…

Here is Scully's call from the 10th inning with the Dodgers down by a run and Kenny Lofton on first.

Now Garciaparra. And for Bochy, more anxious moments. No lead is big enough. Not four in the first. Not five in the last two innings…

And now Seanez, wild…. He's behind three and one, and Bochy is twisting in the wind.

And a high fly ball to left field, it is a way out and gone! The Dodgers win it, 11 to 10!

Oh…un-be-lievable!

Scully took a very long pause as the team celebrated at home plate and the fans went crazy.

I forgot to tell you. The Dodgers are in first place.

Hitless Wonders

Usually when you win a game and check the line score, you'll see, "Four runs, seven hits" or "Six runs, 13 hits." But if you check the Dodgers' box score from their June 29, 2008, 1–0 victory over the Angels, you'll see, "One run, no hits."

Jered Weaver started the game for the Angels, and Chad Billingsley started for the Dodgers in what would turn out to be the wackiest game in their Southland rivalry.

Both pitchers had shutouts going into the fifth, but Weaver was working on a no-hitter. The fifth inning was when you pay attention to such things, so the murmurs of the crowd were building as Weaver took the mound.

Matt Kemp led off and hit a grounder back to Weaver, who bobbled the ball, allowing Kemp to reach first on an error. Two pitches later, Kemp took off for second, and when catcher Jeff Mathis' throw sailed into center field, Kemp took third.

Blake DeWitt then lofted a fly ball to right, scoring Kemp. One run, no hits.

In the bottom of the sixth, Weaver retired Andre Ethier, Russell Martin, and James Loney.

In the top of the seventh, trailing 1–0, the Angels hit for Weaver, who still had a no-hitter but was losing.

In the bottom of the inning, Jose Arredondo came in to pitch and retired Kemp, DeWitt, and Angel Berroa.

In the bottom of the eighth, Arredondo retired Delwyn Young, Juan Pierre, and Ethier. When the Angels failed to score in the top of the ninth, the most lackluster no-hitter in history was over, with the no-hit team picking up the win.

"That is pretty bizarre," manager Joe Torre said after the game.

"This is definitely the craziest game I have ever been a part of," Angels center fielder Torii Hunter said. "I've never been part of a game where you have five hits and give up no hits and you can't get it done."

Only three other times had a pitcher given up no hits but not been credited with a no-hitter because they pitched only eight innings:

June 21, 1890—Charles "Silver" King, Chicago, lost to Brooklyn 1–0

July 1, 1990—Andy Hawkins, New York Yankees, lost to Chicago White Sox 4–0.

April 12, 1992—Matt Young, Boston, lost to Cleveland 2–1.

Mannywood, Manny Did

The Dodgers found themselves hovering around the .500 mark as the 2008 trade deadline approached but still within striking distance of a division title. The feeling was that one big acquisition could push them over the top. There was one big name on the market—Manny Ramirez because the Boston Red Sox had grown tired of his self-aggrandizing act.

Ramirez had a big contract—he was due $21 million—but it was felt that the Red Sox would be willing to pay most of that if someone just took him off their hands.

After a few days of negotiations, the Dodgers announced a monumental deal. They would send Andy LaRoche and Bryan Morris to the Pittsburgh Pirates, who would in turn send Jason Bay to the Boston Red

Dodgers fans hold up a sign that says "MANNYWOOD" for the Dodgers' Manny Ramirez during the sixth inning of a baseball game against the San Francisco Giants on Thursday, April 16, 2009, in Los Angeles. *(AP Photo/Mark J. Terrill)*

Sox. The Red Sox would then send Craig Hansen and Brandon Moss to the Pirates and Ramirez to the Dodgers. The Red Sox also agreed to pay Ramirez for the rest of the season, meaning the Dodgers would essentially be getting him for free.

It was the biggest in-season acquisition the Dodgers had made in years.

"We figured we had to do it," Dodgers general manager Ned Colletti said. "Why would we not do it?"

Why indeed.

Ramirez was a revelation—good-natured, playful, and not at all what was advertised. The guy could hit a little, too.

Manny homered four times in his first six games with the Dodgers, and he became adept at pulling the ball into the left-field seats at Dodger Stadium. It wasn't long before fans seated there started bringing "Mannywood" signs to the game. The Dodgers themselves even installed a "Mannywood" sign on the left-field fence reminiscent of the iconic "Hollywood" sign.

The Dodgers went 30–23 with Ramirez in the lineup and finished the season with an 84–78 record, good enough to win the NL West. Ramirez hit an amazing .396 with 16 homers and 53 RBIs and even finished fourth in NL MVP voting despite playing in only 53 games. But there were still the playoffs to consider, and the Dodgers had failed miserably there since 1988, winning only one game in 12 attempts.

The Dodgers played the Chicago Cubs in the NL Division Series and steamrollered right over them, beating them by scores of 7–2, 10–3, and 3–1. Ramirez hit .500 with two homers and three RBIs.

The train came to a halt during the NL Championship Series against Philadelphia, with the Dodgers losing in five games to the Phillies. (Curse you, Matt Stairs!) Ramirez did more than his fair share, though, hitting .533 with two homers and seven RBIs.

Although the season came to a disappointing end, there was great hope for the future, but only if the Dodgers could re-sign Ramirez, whose contract had expired.

After protracted negotiations, the Dodgers announced on March 9, 2009, that they had signed Ramirez to a two-year, $45 million deal, making him the second-richest player in baseball behind Alex Rodriguez of the New York Yankees.

"Sometimes it's better off to have a two-year deal in a place that you're going to be happy than an eight-year deal in a place you're going to suffer," Ramirez said at the news conference announcing the deal. "I was looking for this place for eight years. Now I'm here. It was a bad economy, and I got a great contract. I won."

Little did anyone realize that the good times of Mannywood were pretty much over.

Dodgers fans went to bed on the night of May 6 with their team in first place with a 21–8 record. Ramirez was hitting .348 with six homers and 20 RBIs. A World Series appearance seemed virtually assured. But every silver lining has a dark cloud. This cloud came out on the morning of May 7 and blotted out the sun for the next 60 days.

Ramirez had tested positive for a female fertility drug that is sometimes used by steroid users to restore testosterone to normal levels. Because of the positive test, Ramirez was suspended for 50 games without pay under baseball's anti-doping policy.

Ramirez blamed the positive test on medication prescribed to him by a doctor for a health issue.

"He gave me a medication, not a steroid, which he thought was okay to give me," Ramirez said in the statement. "Unfortunately, the medication was banned under our drug policy. Under the policy, that mistake is now my responsibility. L.A. is a special place to me, and I know everybody is disappointed. So am I. I'm sorry about this whole situation. I have been advised not to say anything more for now."

A week later, Ramirez addressed his teammates in private.

"It was uncomfortable. He was a little anxious," manager Joe Torre said. "I sensed an uneasiness that I hadn't seen before from Manny. He's remorseful and embarrassed. He just wanted to let the team know how sorry he is for that and for the fact that he's not there for them."

Ramirez returned to the lineup on July 3. There was one more great Mannywood moment left. July 22 was Manny Ramirez bobblehead doll night at Dodger Stadium (the night had been set up before Ramirez was suspended). Nursing an injury, Ramirez wasn't in the lineup.

With the score tied 2–2 and the bases loaded in the sixth, Ramirez was sent up to pinch-hit. Grand slam. Mannywood burned brightly one more time, but he was never the same player. He hit only .269 with 13 homers after coming back from his suspension. The Dodgers made it to the playoffs again, where they swept St. Louis (Ramirez hit .308 with no homers) before losing to Philadelphia once again in the NLCS. Ramirez hit .263 there.

The 2010 season brought more of the same. Ramirez was half the player he used to be, injured often and no longer worth the $25 million he was due. On August 30, he was claimed on waivers by the Chicago White Sox.

"It was probably time for both of us," Colletti said.

The next day, the Mannywood sign was gone. It was as if he had never been there at all.

Loss Takes a Holliday

The Dodgers went into the 2009 playoffs as favorites to win the National League pennant. They finished the season with a 95–67 record and had legendary former Yankees manager Joe Torre as their skipper.

They opened the playoffs against the St. Louis Cardinals in the best-of-five division series. Torre and the Cardinals' Tony La Russa were (and still are) considered two of the best managers of all time, so it figured to be a close series.

The Dodgers won Game 1 at Dodger Stadium 5–3 thanks in part to a two-run homer by Matt Kemp, so things were looking good heading into Game 2. With Games 3 and 4 being played in St. Louis, leaving L.A. with a 2–0 series lead was crucial.

The Cardinals took a 1–0 lead in the top of the second when Matt Holliday homered off Clayton Kershaw. Holliday had been acquired at the trade deadline by the Cardinals, who saw him as the final piece of a World Series–winning puzzle. Holliday responded by hitting .353 and slugging .604 after coming over to the Cardinals.

The Dodgers tied the score in the bottom of the fourth on a solo shot by Andre Ethier only to see the Cardinals retake the lead on a run-scoring double by Colby Rasmus in the seventh inning.

The score stayed 2–1 until the bottom of the ninth inning. Ethier and Manny Ramirez made two quick outs, and when James Loney hit a fly ball to left, it looked like the series would be 1–1 heading back to the Gateway City.

Holliday was a solid defensive player, not quite a Gold Glove–level fielder, but a guy who made the routine plays and occasionally made a spectacular one. This time, Holliday dropped the ball for an error. Actually, the ball missed his glove entirely and hit him in the stomach before dropping to the ground.

"I lost it in the lights," Holliday said after the game. "It's unfortunate timing, it really is, but it wasn't because of lack of effort. I couldn't see the ball. I had it. I was coming in to get it, and then all of a sudden I couldn't see it."

Given new life, the Dodgers responded. Casey Blake drew a clutch walk, fouling off three two-strike pitches before drawing ball four. Ronnie Belliard singled to center to score Juan Pierre ("I just swing at everything I see," Belliard said), who had come in to pinch-run for Loney. A walk to Russell Martin loaded the bases, which brought Mark Loretta to the plate.

Loretta was in the final year of a 15-season major league career and was in the postseason for only the second time. Cardinals closer Ryan Franklin threw him a fastball, the one pitch you should never throw Mark Loretta. He singled to center to win the game, pulling out an unlikely victory from the jaws of defeat.

"That was the best moment of my career," Loretta said.

How unlikely was the win? When Loney hit the fly ball to Holliday, Ethier never saw what happened.

"I had turned my back to the field and was making my way across the dugout," Ethier remembered. "All of a sudden, I heard people go crazy."

CHAPTER 7

THE 2010s

Cy Clone

Some Dodgers fans are convinced that Clayton Kershaw is the second coming of Sandy Koufax (forgetting for a moment that Koufax is alive and well). Others think he must be a genetically engineered facsimile.

How else can you explain the poise and command in one so young?

After three seasons of basically babying Kershaw, watching his pitch counts, making sure he didn't stress his arm too much, the team took the restraints off the left-hander in 2011.

The result was a season for the ages.

In this era of high-octane offenses with every player swinging for the seats, pitchers with low ERAs are rare. While there used to be a handful of 20-game winners every season, you're lucky to get one or two nowadays. Kershaw does them both.

Kershaw was tabbed to start on opening day in 2011 and pitched seven shutout innings against the Giants. Two starts later, 6⅔ shutout innings. Six starts later, seven shutout innings. At the end of June, he was 8–3 with a 2.93 ERA and 128 strikeouts in 116.2 innings.

Watching Kershaw pitch is like watching a great artist paint. He mixes in fastballs with devastating knee-buckling curves, hitting the corners and leaving batters, especially left-handed ones, jelly-legged.

In the second half of the season, Kershaw went 12–1 with a 1.31 ERA. He didn't win 20 games—he won 21. He won the pitching triple crown, leading the league in wins, ERA (2.28), and strikeouts (248).

When it came time to hand out awards, Kershaw collected several, but the big one came on November 17 when he was named the winner of the Cy Young Award, becoming the eighth Dodgers pitcher to win the award.

"A lot of things go through my mind," Kershaw said when told he won. "Just thankful to be a part of it. Undeserving when you see some of the other Dodgers who have won it. I've got a long way to go to have the career those guys did."

Starting pitcher Clayton Kershaw throws against the San Francisco Giants in the eighth inning in San Francisco on Wednesday, July 20, 2011. Los Angeles won the game 1–0, and Kershaw was the winning pitcher. *(AP Photo/Eric Risberg)*

Kershaw was only 23 when he won the award. He received 27 of 32 first-place votes (what were those other five voters thinking?) and easily outdistanced Roy Halladay and Cliff Lee, the two Philadelphia pitchers who finished second and third.

"When I first saw Clayton Kershaw," Vin Scully said, "I didn't have any idea of how great his ability really was. But there was something about him, the way he handled himself. In his first year, in his first few games, it was as if he knew he belonged."

Newcombe. Koufax. Drysdale. Marshall. Valenzuela. Hershiser. Gagne. Yep, Kershaw belongs.

Oh, and about those Kershaw-Koufax comparisons. Don't make them to Kershaw.

"He did it for a long time," Kershaw said in 2013. "He won a lot of awards. He won the World Series. He threw no-hitters. Just a lot of things I'm not even close to accomplishing yet. So I have tremendous respect for him and would never want to put myself in the same category as him."

New Owners in Town

You'll notice that Frank McCourt has not been mentioned a lot in the book. The less said about his tumultuous times as owner, the better. But McCourt did leave the Dodgers a nice parting gift when he sold the team in 2012. He sold it to a group that included NBA legend Magic Johnson.

Johnson is an L.A. icon, not only for being the key member of five Lakers championship teams, but by also being an active member of the community after he retired, becoming a businessman who sought to help those less fortunate.

The Guggenheim Group bought the Dodgers for a record $2.15 billion and was wise enough to know it needed to present a proper public face to Dodgers fans, one they could immediately identify with. The

Group invited Johnson to become a part-owner and asked him to be the ambassador to the fans. Johnson was the perfect pick.

Johnson's first call was to Vin Scully, the most-beloved Dodger of all time. He also reached out to Sandy Koufax, the most-beloved Dodger player of all time, making sure Koufax knew he was welcome with open arms after years of what appeared to be Koufax and the Dodgers distancing themselves from each other.

Then Johnson addressed Dodgers fans, reaching into the past to invoke the name of perhaps the third most-beloved Dodger of all.

"I can't even put into words how it is to be part of this team. But I do know that if there's no Jackie Robinson, I'm not sitting here today."

Johnson became a Dodgers fan when he joined the Lakers in 1979 and could be seen attending several Dodgers games over the years, sitting in the stands with the rest of the fans.

Bay of Puig

The big question from Dodgers fans was, "Could the new owners afford to spend money to upgrade the team?" After all, they just spent $2 billion to buy the team, how much money could they possibly have left?

A lot, it turns out.

"I promise you we'll explore everything. Look, as candid as we can be, we're the Dodgers. We're supposed to be big. We intend to be big. Will we look at big things? You bet," new team president Stan Kasten said. "If the resources involve money, we'll be very flexible."

The first big deal the new owners made turned out to be a notable one. They offered Cuban defector Yasiel Puig a seven-year, $42 million deal to join the team.

"He's got a lot of pluses—power, speed, arm," Dodgers general manager Ned Colletti said. "He's still a lot of a work in progress. He's a very intriguing player."

Because of his defection, Puig had not played baseball in a year when the Dodgers signed him in June 2012. They sent him to the minors where he tore up the league.

"For me, I don't think it will be that difficult to get to the major leagues," Puig said. "This is all about me getting into shape." The Dodgers didn't want to rush him, though, so they left him in the minors throughout the rest of the 2012 season.

In spring training for the 2013 season, Puig was the best player in camp, hitting .526 with three homers and 11 RBIs. With Dodgers fans clamoring for Puig to make the team, the Dodgers sent him to the minors to start the season. They wanted him to solidify his fundamentals.

"I kind of look at Yasiel like a Ferrari," Dodgers manager Don Mattingly said. "The motor's there, the body's there, the wheels are there. Everything's there. We just haven't painted it yet. You leave that out in the sun with no paint, then you get it exposed a little bit."

One June 2, the Dodgers were mired in last place. Yasiel Puig was needed.

In his first game, Puig had two hits and ended the game when he doubled a runner off first with a laser-like throw from the right-field fence.

The Dodgers won 42 of their next 50 games and moved into first place. In June, Puig hit .436 with seven home runs. But his contributions to the team weren't just from his bat, Puig brought a joy and energy to the team that hadn't been seen in years. Every player seemed more involved and took more interest in the team.

The Dodgers were the first team to clinch a playoff spot and were favored to win the World Series before falling to the St. Louis Cardinals in the NLCS.

CHAPTER 8

THE 15 GREATEST L.A. DODGERS OF ALL TIME

In 2012, I conducted a poll asking Dodgers fans to name their 10 greatest L.A. Dodgers of all time. Anyone was eligible for votes, including players, managers, broadcasters, owners, peanut vendors, you name it. First-place votes received 12 points, second place received nine, all the way down to one point for 10th place. There were so many responses to the poll (more than 12,000) that I decided to expand the list to 15 when I announced the results. Here are the 15 greatest Dodgers of all time.

No. 1: Sandy Koufax (6,284 first-place votes, 116,888 points)

Koufax was the first pitcher to win multiple Cy Young Awards, as well as the first pitcher to win a Cy Young Award by a unanimous vote. Many people will tell you that the greatest pitcher in baseball history was Sandy Koufax on four days rest and that the second greatest was Sandy Koufax on three days rest.

Koufax pitched four no-hitters, one of those a perfect game, and led the Dodgers to two World Series titles.

On the L.A. Dodgers' all-time list, Koufax is fourth in wins (156), fourth in strikeouts (2,214), ninth in losses (77), 12th in games pitched (335), third in complete games (133), third in shutouts (38), fourth in walks (709), and second in ERA (2.64).

No. 2: Don Drysdale (471 first-place votes, 73,134 points)

Big D teamed with Sandy Koufax during the 1960s to form one of the most dominating pitching duos in history.

In 1962, Drysdale won 25 games and the Cy Young Award. In 1965, he won 23 games and helped the Dodgers to their third World Series title in L.A. In 1968, he set a record with 58⅓ consecutive scoreless innings, a record that was broken by Orel Hershiser in 1988.

Drysdale was inducted into the Baseball Hall of Fame in 1984, and his No. 53 was retired by the Dodgers that same year.

On the all-time L.A. Dodgers list, Drysdale is third in wins (187), third in strikeouts (2,283), second in losses (152), fourth in games pitched (459), tied for first in complete games (156), second in shutouts (45), third in walks (763), and fourth in ERA (2.98).

No. 3: Vin Scully (3,299 first-place votes, 70,070 points)

When you think of the Dodgers, the first thing that pops into the minds of most people is Vin Scully, the greatest sports broadcaster in history.

Scully joined the Dodgers in 1950, working alongside Radio Hall of Famer and baseball legend Red Barber. In 1976, Dodgers fans voted Scully the "most memorable personality" in Los Angeles Dodgers history.

When the Dodgers moved to L.A. in 1958, they played at the Coliseum, which wasn't really designed for baseball and had some poor sight lines for the fans. Because some fans had such difficulty following

Vin Scully works in his booth at Dodger Stadium in Los Angeles on Sunday, August 22, 2010. *(AP Photo/Jae C. Hong)*

the action there, they began to bring radios to the game and would listen while they were watching it live, a practice that continues to this day at Dodger Stadium.

Here are some of Scully's most memorable calls and quotes (courtesy of baseball-almanac.com):

"All year long they looked to him [Kirk Gibson] to light the fire, and all year long he answered the demands. High fly ball into right field. She is gone! [pause] In a year that has been so improbable, the impossible has happened."

"Sometimes it seems like he's [Bobby Bonilla] playing underwater."

"There's a high bouncer over the mound, over second base, Mantilla's up with it, throws low and wild.... Hodges scores, we go to Chicago! [crowd noise for a nice long while] The Cinderella team [1959 Los Angeles Dodgers] of the National League."

"There's a little roller up along first, behind the bag! It gets through Buckner! Here comes Knight, and the Mets win it!"

"When he [Maury Wills] runs, it's all downhill."

"Andre Dawson has a bruised knee and is listed as day-to-day [pause]. Aren't we all?"

"Football is to baseball as blackjack is to bridge. One is the quick jolt. The other the deliberate, slow-paced game of skill, but never was a sport more ideally suited to television than baseball. It's all there in front of you. It's theater, really. The star is the spotlight on the mound, the supporting cast fanned out around him, the mathematical precision of the game moving with the kind of inevitability of Greek tragedy. With the Greek chorus in the bleachers!"

"He [Bob Gibson] pitches as though he's double-parked."

"He's [Tom Glavine] like a tailor; a little off here, a little off there, and you're done, take a seat."

"How good was Stan Musial? He was good enough to take your breath away."

"It's a mere moment in a man's life between the All-Star Game and an old timers' game."

"It's a passing [the last NBC Game of the Week on October 9, 1989] of a great American tradition. It is sad. I really and truly feel that. It will leave a vast window, to use a Washington word, where people will not get Major League Baseball, and I think that's a tragedy."

"I would come home to listen to a football game—there weren't other sports on—and I would get a pillow and I would crawl under the radio so that the loudspeaker and the roar of the crowd would wash all over me, and I would just get goose bumps like you can't believe. And I knew that of all the things in this world that I wanted, I wanted to be that fella saying, whatever, home run, or touchdown. It just really got to me."

No. 4: Tommy Lasorda (551 first-place votes, 40,298 points)

Lasorda, all the while talking about "bleeding Dodger blue" and "the big Dodger in the sky," compiled a 1,599–1,439 record as Dodgers manager, won two World Series titles (1981, 1988), four National League pennants (1977, 1978, 1981, 1988), and eight division titles (1977, 1978, 1981, 1983, 1985, 1988, 1994, and 1995).

Lasorda was inducted into the Baseball Hall of Fame in 1997 in his first year of eligibility. The Dodgers retired his No. 2 uniform on August 15, 1997.

No. 5: Maury Wills (39,827 points)

Wills is credited by many with bringing the stolen base back to baseball. In his first full season as Dodgers shortstop, Wills led the league with 50 stolen bases, being the first National League player to steal 50 since Max Carey stole 51 in 1923.

In 1962, Wills broke Ty Cobb's 47-year-old record by stealing 104 bases for the Dodgers, and he was named NL Most Valuable Player.

Wills was a five-time All-Star and two-time Gold Glove winner with the Dodgers. On the all-time L.A. Dodgers list, he is fifth in games played (1,593), fourth in hits (1,732), second in runs (876), third in triples (56), 10th in walks (456), and first in stolen bases (490).

No. 6: Steve Garvey (236 first-place votes, 39,277 points)

Some voters thought he was overrated and left him off the ballot entirely; some thought he was the greatest L.A. Dodger of all time.

Steve Garvey was part of the legendary Garvey-Lopes-Russell-Cey infield, which stayed together for almost nine full seasons. Garvey was "Mr. Clean" with the Dodgers, a person far more popular with the fans than with his teammates.

Garvey had six 200-hit seasons with the Dodgers, was an eight-time All-Star, and won four Gold Glove Awards. On the all-time L.A. Dodgers list, Garvey ranks third in games (1,727), second in hits (1,968), third in homers (211), first in doubles (333), first in RBIs (992), sixth in batting average (.301), third in runs (852), is tied for eighth in triples (35) and is 17th in slugging percentage (.459).

No. 7: Orel Hershiser (29,929 points)

Hershiser is on this list for one big reason—almost single-handedly carrying the Dodgers to the 1988 World Series title.

Hershiser ended the regular season by pitching 59 consecutive scoreless innings, breaking the record held by Dodger legend Don Drysdale. Hershiser led the league in wins (23), innings (267), and complete games (15), and was unanimously selected as the Cy Young Award winner after finishing 23–8 with a 2.26 ERA.

In the 1988 NLCS, Hershiser was named the MVP after starting Games 1 and 3, saving Game 4, and pitching a shutout in the decisive Game 7. He then went on to shut down the Oakland A's in the World Series, winning Games 2 and 5 and being named World Series MVP. He is the only player to win the Cy Young Award, the championship series MVP award, and the World Series MVP award in the same season.

On the all-time Dodgers list, Hershiser is seventh in wins (135), fifth in losses (107), 10th in games pitched (353), fifth in games started (309), sixth in strikeouts (1,456), sixth in complete games (65), sixth in innings pitched (2,180.2), sixth in walks allowed (667), sixth in shutouts (24), and 10th in ERA (3.12).

No. 8: Fernando Valenzuela (79 first-place votes, 29,693 points)

Before Mannywood, before Nomomania, there was the original and the best—Fernandomania.

After an injury to Jerry Reuss prevented him from starting the Dodgers' 1981 season opener, the Dodgers turned to 20-year-old rookie Fernando Valenzuela. He pitched a shutout, and Fernandomania was off and running. Valenzuela began the season 8–0 with five shutouts, and he was the runaway winner of the Rookie of the Year Award and the Cy Young Award after finishing 13–7 with a 2.48 ERA.

Valenzuela's last great season with the Dodgers was in 1986 when he went 21–11 with a 3.14 ERA. In that year's All-Star Game, he tied a record by striking out five consecutive batters.

Valenzuela's last great moment with the team came against the St. Louis Cardinals on June 29, 1990, when he pitched his first and only no-hitter. He was released by the Dodgers during spring training in 1991.

On the all-time Dodgers list, Valenzuela is sixth in wins (141), fifth in strikeouts (1,759), fourth in losses (116), 13th in games (331), fourth in complete games (107), fifth in innings pitched (2,348.2), second in walks (915), and fifth in shutouts (29).

No. 9: Mike Piazza (24,117 points)

The best-hitting catcher in baseball history, Piazza was drafted by the Dodgers in the 62nd round of the 1988 first-year player draft and the

1,390ᵗʰ player picked overall. The pick was a favor to Tommy Lasorda, who is the godfather to one of Piazza's brothers.

Piazza came up to the team at the end of 1992 and really came into his own in 1993 when he won the Rookie of the Year Award after hitting .318 with 35 home runs (including two on the last day of the season when the Dodgers prevented the Giants from reaching the playoffs) and 112 RBIs.

Piazza hit .319, .346, .336, and .362 in his next four seasons before one of the most reviled trades in Dodgers history took place on May 14, 1998. Piazza was traded, along with Todd Zeile, to the Florida Marlins for Gary Sheffield, Charles Johnson, Bobby Bonilla, Jim Eisenreich, and Manuel Barrios. Several people who voted said that the day Piazza was traded was the day they stopped being a Dodgers fan.

Piazza went on to have several great seasons with the New York Mets, and he recently stated that if he is elected to the Hall of Fame, he wants to go in as a Met. Which is exactly what he did when he was enshrined in 2016.

On the L.A. Dodgers all-time list, Piazza is fifth in homers (177), 11ᵗʰ in RBIs (563), first in batting average (.331), and second in slugging percentage (.572).

No. 10: Don Sutton (20,503 points)

Don Sutton pitched for the Dodgers from 1966 to 1980 and in 1988, and he is the team's all-time wins leader. He finished in the top five of Cy Young Award voting every year from 1972 to 1976 and won the ERA title in 1980. Sutton pitched for the Astros, Brewers, A's, and Angels from 1981 to 1987 before returning to the Dodgers in their 1988 World Series title year. Sutton was released in August of that season and did not appear in the playoffs.

On the L.A. Dodgers all-time list, Sutton ranks first in wins (233), losses (181), games started (533), innings (3,816.1), and shutouts (52).

Don Sutton pitches in the 48th All-Star Game at Yankee Stadium in New York on Tuesday, July 20, 1977. Sutton, who pitched the first three innings, was named Most Valuable Player. *(AP Photo)*

He's second in games (550) and strikeouts (2,696). He is tied for first in complete games (156) and is seventh in ERA (3.09).

No. 11 Walter Alston (16,306 points)

Pretty much the complete opposite of Tommy Lasorda as far as personality goes, Walt Alston was nonetheless one of the most successful managers in Dodgers history.

Alston began managing the Dodgers in 1954 when they were still in Brooklyn, and he remained manager until 1976, winning seven NL pennants (1955, 1956, 1959, 1963, 1965, 1966, 1974) and four World Series titles, (1955, 1959, 1963, 1965), three of them in Los Angeles.

Alston retired with a final record of 2,040–1,613. He had his No. 24 retired by the team in 1977, and he was elected to the Baseball Hall of Fame in 1983.

Alston died at the age of 72 on October 1, 1984.

No. 12: Ron Cey (12,804 points)

The Dodgers made the World Series in 1974, 1977, 1978, and 1981, and it would be hard to find a player more responsible for that than Ron Cey. Steve Garvey got most of the publicity (and MVP votes), but Cey's combination of power, walks (his lower batting averages masked one of the higher on-base percentages on the team each season), and defense made him a key member of the Dodgers.

Cey, however, will probably always be best known for his nickname "Penguin," given to him because of his unique running style, which was a result of his knees seemingly being the same distance from the ground as a five-year-old kid.

Traded to the Cubs before the 1983 season for Vance Lovelace, Cey led the Cubs to the 1984 playoffs, too.

On the L.A. Dodgers' all-time list, Cey is sixth in games played (1,481), sixth in hits (1,378), second in homers (228), eighth in doubles (223), fourth in runs batted in (842), seventh in runs scored (715), and first in walks (765).

No. 13: Walter O'Malley (157 first-place votes, 11,076 points)

O'Malley received the sixth most first-place votes but finished 13th because he was left off many ballots entirely. Those who did vote for him mainly had the same reason—if he hadn't moved the team, there would be no L.A. Dodgers to vote for at all.

He made the decision to move the Dodgers from Brooklyn to L.A. in time for the 1958 season. He did not have a stadium ready for the Dodgers, so he rented the Coliseum for $200,000 per year for 1958 and 1959, plus 10 percent of the ticket revenue. The team moved to Dodger Stadium in 1962, and the rest, as they say, is history.

O'Malley is not without his detractors, however, including many people in Brooklyn who still curse his name for moving the Dodgers away, and some people in L.A. who feel they were unfairly forced from their homes to make way for Dodger Stadium.

No. 14: Tommy Davis (9,741 points)

Davis hit .346 in 1962 and won the National League batting crown, led the league with 230 hits, and set a Dodgers record with 153 runs batted in. He won the batting title again in 1963 with a .326 average, and he is still the last Dodgers player to win a batting title. In the 1963 World Series, Davis hit .400 as the Dodgers swept the New York Yankees, with Davis driving in the game's only run in the 1–0 victory in Game 3.

On May 1, 1965, against the visiting Giants, he broke and dislocated his ankle sliding into second base while trying to break up a double play and was lost for the remainder of the season. He hit .313 in 1966 and was traded to the New York Mets on November 29, 1966, for Jim Hickman and Ron Hunt.

On the L.A. Dodgers' career list, Davis is fifth in batting average (.304) and 18th in RBIs (465).

No. 15: Kirk Gibson (7,306 points)

Gibson joined the Dodgers, who were coming off two losing seasons, in 1988 and almost immediately made his presence felt. In spring training, relief pitcher Jesse Orosco smeared shoe polish on the inside of Gibson's cap, leaving Gibson's forehead smeared with it when he wore his cap during an exhibition game. Realizing what had happened, Gibson immediately pulled himself from the game and tore into his teammates afterward for their lack of professionalism, telling them he now knew why they had been losers for the last two seasons.

Gibson quickly became the leader of the team and won the NL MVP Award for the season after batting .290 with 25 home runs, 76 RBIs, 106 runs, and 31 stolen bases. This only set the stage for one of the most remarkable home runs in baseball history.

Gibson began Game 1 of the World Series on the bench because of injuries to both legs. With the Dodgers trailing 4–3 in the bottom of the ninth and Mike Davis on first, Gibson came up as a pinch-hitter, facing the best closer in baseball, Dennis Eckersley of Oakland. Unable to catch up to Eckersley's fastball, Gibson quickly fell behind 0–2 in the count but fouled off several pitches and worked the count full.

Remembering a scouting report by Mel Didier that said Eckersley would throw a backdoor slider on a full count, Gibson homered, giving the Dodgers a dramatic 5–4 victory.

Gibson spent only three seasons with the Dodgers, and it is his World Series homer that put him in 15th place ahead of many Dodgers who had been with the team much longer but never had a moment half as memorable.

EPILOGUE

A lot has happened in the ensuing years. Let's get right to it.

Don Mattingly Out; Dave Roberts In

The Dodgers made the postseason in 2014 and 2015, but lost in the NLDS both times and appeared to be unable to get over that NLDS hurdle. The Guggenheim Group (which bought the team in 2012) and manager Don Mattingly mutually agreed to part ways after the 2015 season, with one year left on his contract.

"As our end-of-season process began, we discussed the past year, our future goals, necessary changes, roster needs, and other matters relating to next year's campaign," Dodgers president of baseball operations Andrew Friedman said. "As the dialogue progressed daily, it evolved to a point where we all agreed that it might be best for both sides to start fresh. We decided to think about it for a couple of days and when we spoke again, we felt comfortable that this was the direction to go.

"I have the utmost respect for Donnie and thoroughly enjoyed working with him this past season. I want to thank him for his hard work and collaboration, as well as his accomplishments, including three consecutive National League West titles. I wish him nothing but success in the future."

Mattingly managed the Dodgers for five seasons, and while most fans viewed him as a Yankee and never really warmed to him, he went 446–363 at the helm, winning the 2013 NLDS, but losing in the 2013 NLCS, the 2014 NLDS, and the 2015 NLDS. Even Mattingly seemed to think it was time for a change.

"I'm honored and proud to have had the opportunity to manage the Los Angeles Dodgers. I've enjoyed my experiences and relationships with the organization's staff and players throughout my eight years in L.A.

"After meeting with Andrew, we all felt that a fresh start would be good for both the organization and me. We talked about several scenarios, including my returning in 2016. However, I believe this is the right

Manager Dave Roberts celebrates with third baseman Justin Turner after defeating the San Diego Padres 4–3 on May 3, 2019, in San Diego. *(AP Photo/ Gregory Bull)*

time and right move for both parties. I'm still very passionate about managing and hope to get the opportunity in the near future. In the meantime, I want to thank the Dodger organization, the city, and our fans for the opportunity and wish the club well going forward."

The immediate question for Dodgers fans: Who would replace Mattingly? The Dodgers had had only nine managers since moving to L.A. for the 1958 season. Who would be the next man up?

Gabe Kapler. The Dodgers seemed all set to hire him. But wait! They decided to conduct one more interview. And in walked Dave Roberts, a former Dodger best known for the stolen base in Game 4 of the 2004 ALCS that led to a Boston Red Sox victory, catapulting them to an amazing 4–3 series win over the dreaded New York Yankees.

By all accounts, Roberts just blew everyone away in his interview for the job, and it was quickly decided that he would be the next manager.

"The Dodgers are the groundbreaking franchise of Jackie Robinson, Roy Campanella, Sandy Koufax, Maury Wills, Fernando Valenzuela, and Hideo Nomo," Roberts said. "When I put on this uniform as a player, I understood the special responsibility to honor those that played before me as well as the amazing bond between the Dodgers and their fans. I feel that I have now come full circle in my career and there is plenty of unfinished business left in L.A."

Roberts has since managed the Dodgers to three World Series appearances and one title, along with the best winning percentage of any manager in MLB history. Many Dodgers fans are still down on him, because sometimes his pitcher decisions are odd. Then again, some people would view the *Mona Lisa* and complain it's too small.

The Rise and Fall of Yasiel Puig

As recounted previously in this book, Yasiel Puig was a sensation when he first came up to the Dodgers. He seemed to be able to do anything: hit for average, hit for power, run, field and throw. And his joyous demeanor made it an instant love affair with fans.

But then you started hearing some anonymous grumbling. He wasn't a team player. He often showed up late. He didn't pay attention on defense.

Puig's hitting began to suffer. He went from being an elite hitter to one who was a bit above average. Fans would rave over his ability to run seemingly a mile to catch a ball, or to dive and just miss it. Teammates would say that if he had paid attention to the scouting reports and the coaches, he would have been in position to catch the ball without having to run. What looked like a great play to fans was in fact a poor play.

But even with all of that, the hearts of some fans were broken on December 21, 2018, when the Dodgers traded Puig, along with Matt Kemp, left-hander Alex Wood, catcher Kyle Farmer, and $7 million to the Cincinnati Reds for right-hander Homer Bailey, minor-league infielder Jeter Downs, and minor-league right-hander Josiah Gray.

It was the end of an era. When asked his opinion of Puig's Dodger tenure, Friedman said, "That is a very deep question."

Justin Turner on Puig, to *Los Angeles Times* Dodgers reporter Andy McCullough in 2019: "The frustrating part is that if Puig was good, and played good, then we would be a really, really, really good team. So everyone wanted him to be that good player. He didn't see it that way. He just saw it as he was just going to show up and do whatever he wants."

Puig went from Cincinnati to Cleveland and was out of the majors when no one signed him after the 2019 season. A big reason for that was Puig's confession that he didn't try hard on defense, telling Cincinnati reporters, "The last couple of years, I didn't work hard because I still have a contract to go. Now, I think work harder than any year of my life."

Puig is currently playing in Korea and says his attitude has changed. Let's hope he gets one more chance to prove it.

Vin Scully Retires and Passes Away

The build up to the 2016 season was marred by some bad news that fans knew would come eventually, they just hoped not for a while. Legendary Dodgers broadcaster Vin Scully was going to retire after the season, after only 67 seasons on the job. To put that in perspective, if Joe Davis, the man who succeeded Scully, broadcasts for 67 seasons, his last season will be in 2084.

And then, just as we were finally getting over him not being in the booth, we got the tragic news in August 2022 that Scully died at the age of 94.

Broadcasters Orel Hershiser (left) and Joe Davis unveil a banner during a ceremony to honor the memory of Vin Scully prior to a game on Friday, August 5, 2022, three days after Scully passed away. *(AP Photo/Mark J. Terrill)*

"We have lost an icon," Dodgers president and CEO Stan Kasten said. "Vin Scully was one of the greatest voices in all of sports. He was a giant of a man, not only as a broadcaster, but as a humanitarian. He loved people. He loved life. He loved baseball and the Dodgers. And he loved his family. His voice will always be heard and etched in all of our minds forever."

One of the amazing things about Vin was his timing. It was like he could peek into the future and see how long an at-bat was going to last. He'd start a story about a batter, and you'd think, "He's never going to finish this story before this guy gets a hit or makes an out. But lo and behold, every time the story would wrap up right before the batter was retired or got on base. It was incredible. How did he know?

I was fortunate enough to meet Scully twice. Once was backstage at a televised event called "Scully and Wooden: For the Kids," where

Scully and former UCLA basketball coach John Wooden told stories at an event that raised money for charity. Backstage, I was introduced to Scully, who immediately said my name: "Houston Mitchell, what a pleasure to meet you." All I could think was, "Vin Scully just said my name." I said something back that was probably dumb, Scully laughed politely and we both moved on to other things.

After the event, I'm just standing there doing nothing, when who comes up from behind me but Vin. "Houston Mitchell, and it seems right that I call you by your whole name, those were some great questions you came up with. Thank you so much for helping make me look good out there." He shook my hand, gave me a wink, and then was gone, like Santa Claus disappearing up the chimney.

Six years later, I'm writing the first edition of this book and I'm hoping I can talk to Vin so he can tell me some Jim Gilliam stories I can use. I call the Dodgers, and they let me know that I can have five minutes with Vin if I get there three hours before the following night's game. But they stress he is very busy and can only give me five minutes. No problem.

I get there and wait, and Vin is brought over to me. I tell him what I'm doing and hope he can talk about Gilliam. He says, "We met at the Wooden event, didn't we?" I was surprised he remembered, but he did. We sit at a table and he tells me a story about Gilliam that is recounted in this book. The five minutes are up and someone from the Dodgers comes over to very politely shepherd him away. He stops them and says, "I'm not done with my story, give me a few more minutes" The person leaves. Vin spends about 30 minutes telling me several stories about Gilliam and others. The person from the Dodgers comes to get him again. Vin looks at me and says, "Do you have everything you need?" I say yes, and he says, "Houston Mitchell, always a pleasure to talk to you."

They say never meet your heroes, but in this case I'm glad I did.

Normally I would recap his career and talk about how great he was. How we all fell asleep listening to him on the radio and how he, Jackie Robinson, and Fernando Valenzuela created more Dodgers fans than any other people in history. But you know all of that. One thing I learned in writing the Dodgers newsletter for *The Times* is that each Dodger fan had some sort of individual connection with Vin. When he retired, and later when he died, I was flooded with emails from fans who shared those stories. So instead of preaching to the choir on Vin's greatness, I'm going to let Vin have the stage and repeat the final words he said as a Dodgers broadcaster:

"You know, friends, so many people have wished me congratulations on a 67-year career in baseball, and they've wished me a wonderful retirement with my family. And now, all I can do is tell you what I wish for you.

"May God give you, for every storm, a rainbow; for every tear, a smile; for every care, a promise; and a blessing in each trial. For every problem life sends, a faithful friend to share; for every sigh, a sweet song; and an answer for each prayer.

"You and I have been friends for a long time, but I know in my heart that I've always needed you more than you've needed me, and I'll miss our time together more than I can say.

"But you know what, there will be a new day, and eventually a new year. And when the upcoming winter gives way to spring, rest assured it will be time for Dodger baseball.

"So this is Vin Scully, wishing you a very pleasant good afternoon, wherever you may be."

Thank you, Vin, for everything.

Walk It Off

Justin Turner grew up a Dodgers fan and studied Dodger history. And in the second game of the 2017 NLCS, he became part of Dodgers history.

The Dodgers were taking on the defending champions Cubs, the team that defeated L.A. in the 2016 NLCS.

The Dodgers won Game 1, 5–2, but Game 2 was a tense affair, tied 1–1 going into the bottom of the ninth. Cubs reliever Brian Duensing, who had pitched a scoreless eighth inning, stayed in to pitch the bottom of the ninth. He walked Yasiel Puig, gave up a sacrifice bunt to Charlie Culberson, and struck out Kyle Farmer. Joe Maddon came to the mound, and most assumed he'd be bringing in closer Wade Davis. Instead, in came John Lackey, a starter who had made only six relief appearances during his 15-year career. He walked Chris Taylor to put runners at first and second. Up to the plate stepped Turner. The second pitch he saw was a 92-mph fastball that moved to the center of the plate.

Turner launched it to centerfield, where a fan caught it. Turner didn't see that though, he was rounding the bases after a game-winning homer that sent the Dodger Stadium crowd into pandemonium.

Turner: "That was the coolest thing I've ever done in my baseball career. I felt like I was floating around the bases."

And his teammates knew the game was over when Turner stepped up.

Austin Barnes: "That's the guy we want up there."

Chris Taylor: "He's probably the most clutch player I've ever played with."

To make it even more memorable, Turner hit the homer on the 29th anniversary of Kirk Gibson's iconic World Series Game 1 home run.

"One of my earliest baseball memories was being at my grandma's house and watching that game and watching Gibby hit that homer," Turner said to the assembled media after the game. "I can't even put it into words right now. It's incredible. The most important thing was, obviously, helping us get another win. But that's something down the road, hopefully many, many years from now, I'll get to tell stories about."

Stolen: One World Series Title

That 2017 Dodgers seemed like a team of destiny. They led baseball with 104 wins. Cody Bellinger came out of nowhere to hit 39 homers, win the Rookie of the Year Award, and finish in the top 10 in MVP voting. Eight players hit at least 10 homers. Clayton Kershaw went 18–4 with a 2.31 ERA and finished second in Cy Young voting. Kenley Jansen had a 1.32 ERA to go with 41 saves to finish fifth in Cy Young voting. There were numerous come-from-behind victories that sent Dodger fans home deliriously happy, including one where the Dodgers hit three straight homers to tie the score in the bottom of the ninth, then won on a pinch-hit single by Adrian Gonzalez.

Every Dodger fan knew this was the year. The team steamrolled through the NL playoffs, beating Arizona 3–0 and the defending champion Cubs 4–1. The only thing left to do was play the Houston Astros to claim what was rightfully theirs.

But a funny thing happened. They lost in seven games. And sometimes it seemed the Astros knew what pitches were coming. But that was just conspiratorial thinking, right?

And then someone on YouTube put up video that showed you could hear a banging noise when Astros hitters were at the plate and a breaking pitch was coming. Coincidence, right?

Coincidence that the Astros scored 18 runs on 26 hits and six home runs in two series-changing victories at Minute Maid Park?

And then video went up of this noise happening all through the season, always when a breaking pitch was coming. A former Astros pitcher said they were indeed cheating. It got so bad, MLB launched an investigation.

Three years later, the investigation concluded. The nine-page commissioner's report detailed how the Astros stole catchers' signs throughout the 2017 season by picking them up on a television feed and relaying them to batters by banging on a trash can.

MLB suspended Astros general manager Jeff Luhnow and manager A.J. Hinch for one year. The Astros decided to fire them instead. The team was also fined $5 million and was stripped of first- and second-round draft picks in 2020 and 2021.

But the Astros were allowed to keep their title. No players were punished. It continues to be a black mark against the game of baseball.

And the Astros will forever be known as the Houston Asterisks.

Perhaps Cody Bellinger and Justin Turner put it best:

"Everybody knows they stole the ring from us," Bellinger said.

"Now any player who goes forward and cheats to win a World Series," Turner said, "they can live with themselves knowing that, 'Oh, it's okay… it's just the GM and manager losing their jobs. I still get to be called a champion the rest of my life.'"

Longest World Series Game Ever

If you were there, you'll never forget it. If you were watching at home, you'll never forget staring longingly at your bed while Game 3 of the 2018 World Series refused to end.

The Boston Red Sox had a 2–0 Series lead and the Dodgers needed a victory. Game 3 started at 5:12 PM Pacific Time on a beautiful late afternoon at Dodger Stadium. Thanks to a masterful pitching performance by Walker Buehler and a home run by Joc Pederson, the Dodgers led 1–0 going into the top of the eighth.

Manager Dave Roberts brought in closer Kenley Jansen in an attempt to get a two-inning save. Two outs later, Jackie Bradley Jr. homered to tie the score, 1–1. It stayed that way into the 10th inning.

And into the 11th inning.

And into the 12th inning.

It looked like the game would end in the 13th inning. Boston's Brock Holt started it off with a walk and then stole second. He scored on

Eduardo Nunez's single when Scott Alexander, trying to make a throw he shouldn't have, threw the ball past first for an error. The Red Sox loaded the bases with two out, but didn't score again.

Max Muncy (his name becomes important later), was walked by Nathan Eovaldi to lead off the bottom of the inning. He stayed at first when Manny Machado flew out to left, then advanced to second when Nunez had to make a difficult catch in foul territory, crashing into the stands. When Yasiel Puig hit a grounder to second, it looked like the game was over. But Ian Kinsler slipped while throwing and the ball skipped past first, allowing Muncy to score. It was now 2–2 heading into the 14th.

And it was 2–2 heading into the 15th.

And 2–2 heading into the 16th.

And (stop me if you've heard this before) 2–2 heading into the 17th.

Finally, the 18th began, making Game 3 the equivalent of a doubleheader.

Alex Wood retired the Red Sox in order in the top of the 18th and Eovaldi trotted to the mound to begin his seventh inning in relief. Muncy worked the count full, then homered to give the Dodgers a 3–2 win. What was left of the crowd let out an exhausted cheer and then staggered to their cars.

Muncy on the homer: "The feeling was pure joy and excitement. That's about all I can think of, because it's hard to describe how good a feeling it is. As the game kept going, you look up and see the 18th inning, and you're like, 'Holy cow, where did the game go?' Those last nine innings or so just kind of blended together."

It ended the longest game in World Series history at seven hours and 20 minutes. The teams combined to throw 561 pitches. The game took longer to play than the entire 1939 World Series, which had seven hours and five minutes of game time in four games.

Unfortunately, the Red Sox won the next two games, taking a bit of the edge off the thrill of the Game 3 win. Either way though, it was "a hell of a game," as Kiké Hernandez put it.

Chris Taylor Sends Them Home Happy

The 2021 Dodgers won 106 games, the second-best record in the majors. Unfortunately, the San Francisco Giants won 107 games and beat them for the division title. That meant that the Dodgers would have to play a winner-take-all wild-card game against the St. Louis Cardinals to determine who would advance to the NLDS to face… the Giants.

Chris Taylor had a dreadful second half for the Dodgers in 2021. He had a neck injury that limited his range of motion at the plate and he hit .223/.290/.419 after the All-Star break, far below his usual numbers. He was on the bench when the wild-card game began.

The Cardinals got a run off of Max Scherzer in the top of the first, but the Dodgers tied it in the fourth on a home run by Justin Turner. Taylor came into the game in the top of the seventh to play left field, setting the stage for a dramatic ninth inning.

Cardinals reliever T.J. McFarland got two quick outs before walking Cody Bellinger. With Taylor coming to the plate, the Cardinals brought in right-hander Alex Reyes to pitch. On his fourth pitch, Taylor hit the ball into the left-field bleachers. He raised a fist in the air as he rounded the bases, greeted by a mass of Dodgers humanity at home plate.

"You might not start the game, but you can impact the game," Dave Roberts said. "And Chris Taylor won us the game tonight."

"These are the type of moments you dream about and live for," Taylor said. "Honestly, I was just trying to hit a single, not trying to do too much, and he gave me a good slider to hit and I was able to get it up in the air. I was trying to keep things small; think small, big things happens. I'll be able to look back on this the rest of my life."

Champions Again

It will be interesting to see how history treats the 2020 season. Right now, fresh in our minds, it doesn't seem too bizarre. But in 25 years, will people look back at a 60-game season and wonder what happened? Will COVID be a distant memory by then?

Teams reported for Spring Training that year, but not long after, the COVID pandemic caused the postponement of the season. It was eventually decided to begin the season on July 23, with teams playing in empty stadiums (COVID protocols did not allow for gatherings of more than 50 people) and with teams playing only within their own divisions.

Several teams came up with the idea of fans sending in photos to create cardboard cutouts, which were placed in stadiums to give the illusion of fans being in attendance. At Dodger Stadium, you could see cardboard cutouts of Vin Scully, Larry David, and George Lopez near each other.

The Dodgers went 43–17 during the season, the best record in baseball. Because of the short season, MLB allowed eight teams from each league to make the postseason.

Milwaukee, which finished under .500, did not provide much of a challenge in the opening round, with the Dodgers sweeping the Brewers. The Padres were swept out of the playoffs in the next round, setting up an NLCS matchup with the Atlanta Braves.

COVID protocols had relaxed slightly by this time. The NLCS was played at Globe Life Field in Arlington, Texas, home of the Rangers, before a limited number of fans.

The Dodgers were pushed to the brink of elimination by a group of inexperienced starters who had a 2.58 ERA and were 8–1 in the Braves' first nine postseason games. The Braves won the first two games, but the

The Dodgers celebrate after defeating the Tampa Bay Rays 3–1 in Game 6 to win the World Series in Arlington, Texas. *(AP Photo/Tony Gutierrez)*

Dodgers seemed to turn the tide after dealing Atlanta an embarrassing 15–3 defeat in Game 3. But they fell behind 3–1 after losing Game 4.

Then the Dodgers took over. Will Smith's three-run homer erased the Dodgers' Game 5 deficit.

The Dodgers scored three runs in the first inning of Game 6 and cruised to victory behind Walker Buehler.

Cody Bellinger delivered the winning run in Game 7, his solo shot in the seventh inning breaking a tie created by Kiké Hernández's pinch-hit solo shot in the sixth.

That brought the Dodgers to their third World Series in four seasons. The Tampa Bay Rays were the opponent after defeating the Houston Asterisks in the ALCS, preventing a matchup that Dodger fans were anticipating and dreading at the same time. The Dodgers were heavily favored, but the Rays proved they belonged, pushing the Dodgers to six games.

Finally, after 32 years, the title was claimed on October 27.

Facing elimination in Game 6, the Rays started their ace, Blake Snell, against Tony Gonsolin for L.A. The Rays scored in the first inning on a solo homer by Randy Arozarena. The game was quiet after that until something inexplicable happened.

Snell gave up a hit to Austin Barnes with one out in the bottom of the sixth inning and Rays manager Kevin Cash decided to remove Snell. Keep in mind that Snell was their best starter and had given up only two hits in 5.1 innings, striking out nine and walking none. Cash brought in Nick Anderson, who gave up a double to Mookie Betts and then threw a wild pitch that allowed Barnes to score the tying run. Corey Seager hit a grounder that scored Betts. The Dodgers scored again in the eighth on Betts' homer. Julio Urías closed it out by striking out Willy Adames looking, as the Dodgers won their seventh World Series title and first since 1988.

"I've been saying 'World Series champs' in my head over and over again," Clayton Kershaw said afterward. "I can't put it into words yet. I'm just so, so thankful to be a part of this group of guys, and so very thankful that we get to be on the team that is bringing back a World Series to Dodger fans after 32 years. They've waited for a long time.

"We won a World Series!" Kershaw yelled. "I can't believe it. It just feels good to say. I'm gonna keep saying it a few more times."

Kenley Jansen, who had lost his role as closer at the end of the season, had the unfamiliar role of watching as someone else closed out an important Dodger victory. But he remained classy.

"It's a team, man. I'm ready any time the phone rings. Yes, we all want that moment, but Julio was throwing ball really well, and that's awesome. I feel like I'm a true Dodger now. After 32 years, the trophy going back to L.A. It's an awesome feeling. I will cherish and remember this moment my whole life."

ACKNOWLEDGMENTS

This book wouldn't be possible without the help of several people.

First, I want to thank the many Dodgers who answered questions in person or via email over the last couple of years: Dave Anderson, Tim Belcher, Ron Cey, Chuck Essegian, Steve Garvey, Kirk Gibson, Alfredo Griffin, Shawn Green, Mickey Hatcher, Orel Hershiser, Ricky Horton, Lou Johnson, Tim Leary, Davey Lopes, Mike Marshall, Bill Russell, Steve Sax, Mike Scioscia, John Shelby, Franklin Stubbs, Derrel Thomas, Tracy Woodson, and Steve Yeager.

There are a handful of former Dodgers who need to be singled out.

Jerry Reuss was kind enough to answer several questions about his no-hitter and about the 1981 Dodgers. He took the time to answer each question carefully, and his insights made this book much better. I thank him for that.

Fred Claire answered many questions and was always a valuable resource whenever I needed something clarified, or as I now refer to it, Claire-ified. His kindness will not be forgotten.

Ross Porter has been a friend for several years now. Not only did he contribute greatly to this book, I was honored when he agreed to write the foreword. It's easy to get lost working alongside Vin Scully, but Ross carved a niche all his own in Dodger history. The warm reception he receives when he returns to the Stadium is testament to the goodness of the man and the respect people have for him.

The last Dodger I have to thank is Vin Scully. It's not often I get nervous when making an interview request, but when I asked if I could interview Scully, I was on pins and needles until I got the response: "Sure." I went down to Dodger Stadium before a game near the end of the 2013 season, all set for a quick five-minute interview. Five minutes turned into 20 as Scully told wonderful stories about Don Drysdale and Jim Gilliam, two men who needed to be part of this book. To me, interviewing Scully legitimized this entire project, because if you don't talk to the greatest Dodger of them all, then you don't have much of a book. I will never be able to repay his generosity of time.

Dodgers front-office personnel Mark Langill and Garrett Thomas helped me line up interviews of Dodgers I couldn't track down myself. Thank you for that. Josh Rawitch, who worked for the team before moving over to the Arizona Diamondbacks, provided helpful guidance. And Josh also made my youngest daughter, Hannah, feel like the biggest Dodgers fan of all. Thank you, Josh.

This work stands on the backs of many of my past and present colleagues at the *Times*. To name just a few: Paul Zimmerman, Frank Finch, Ross Newhan, Mark Heisler, Earl Gustkey, Dan Hafner, Bill Plaschke, Paul Gutierrez, T.J. Simers, Dylan Hernandez, Mike DiGiovanna, Bob Nightengale, Jerry Crowe, Jim Murray, Alan Malamud, Gary Klein, and Steve Dilbeck.

The folks at Triumph Books took a chance on this first-time author, and I am eternally grateful for that. I hope their confidence has paid off. I especially want to thank Tom Bast, who was my first contact at Triumph, and Karen O'Brien, whose editing made this book twice as good as it would have been.

To my good friend Emilio Garcia-Ruiz, thanks for always encouraging me to write and never letting me give up on my goals.

To my brother, who took me to tons of baseball games when I was a kid and enhanced my love of the game (even if they were mostly Angels games).

To my kids, Sabrina, Samantha, and Hannah: without even realizing it, you three remind me every day just what is important in life—family. If there are three better daughters in the world, I'd like to hear about them.

Finally, to my wife, Diana, who is my biggest supporter and best friend. This book would mean nothing without you. You have filled my days with happiness and taught me what being a real man is all about. I love you very much.

APPENDIX

The Dodgers' record each season since moving to Los Angeles:

Year	Team	Record	Place	Best Player	Manager
1958	Los Angeles Dodgers	71–83	7th of 8	Don Drysdale	Walter Alston
1959	Los Angeles Dodgers	88–68	1st of 8	Don Drysdale	Walter Alston
1960	Los Angeles Dodgers	82–72	4th of 8	Don Drysdale	Walter Alston
1961	Los Angeles Dodgers	89–65	2nd of 8	Don Drysdale	Walter Alston
1962	Los Angeles Dodgers	102–63	2nd of 10	Maury Wills	Walter Alston
1963	Los Angeles Dodgers	99–63	1st of 10	Sandy Koufax	Walter Alston
1964	Los Angeles Dodgers	80–82	6th of 10	Willie Davis	Walter Alston
1965	Los Angeles Dodgers	97–65	1st of 10	Sandy Koufax	Walter Alston
1966	Los Angeles Dodgers	95–67	1st of 10	Sandy Koufax	Walter Alston
1967	Los Angeles Dodgers	73–89	8th of 10	Don Drysdale	Walter Alston
1968	Los Angeles Dodgers	76–86	7th of 10	Tom Haller	Walter Alston
1969	Los Angeles Dodgers	85–77	4th of 6	Claude Osteen	Walter Alston
1970	Los Angeles Dodgers	87–74	2nd of 6	Billy Grabarkewitz	Walter Alston
1971	Los Angeles Dodgers	89–73	2nd of 6	Dick Allen	Walter Alston
1972	Los Angeles Dodgers	85–70	2nd of 6	Don Sutton	Walter Alston
1973	Los Angeles Dodgers	95–66	2nd of 6	Don Sutton	Walter Alston
1974	Los Angeles Dodgers	102–60	1st of 6	Jim Wynn	Walter Alston
1975	Los Angeles Dodgers	88–74	2nd of 6	Andy Messersmith	Walter Alston
1976	Los Angeles Dodgers	92–70	2nd of 6	Ron Cey	Walter Alston
1977	Los Angeles Dodgers	98–64	1st of 6	Reggie Smith	Tom Lasorda
1978	Los Angeles Dodgers	95–67	1st of 6	Ron Cey	Tom Lasorda
1979	Los Angeles Dodgers	79–83	3rd of 6	Ron Cey	Tom Lasorda
1980	Los Angeles Dodgers	92–71	2nd of 6	Don Sutton	Tom Lasorda
1981*	Los Angeles Dodgers	63–47	1st/3rd of 6	Fernando Valenzuela	Tom Lasorda
1982	Los Angeles Dodgers	88–74	2nd of 6	Pedro Guerrero	Tom Lasorda
1983	Los Angeles Dodgers	91–71	1st of 6	Pedro Guerrero	Tom Lasorda
1984	Los Angeles Dodgers	79–83	4th of 6	Alejandro Pena	Tom Lasorda
1985	Los Angeles Dodgers	95–67	1st of 6	Pedro Guerrero	Tom Lasorda
1986	Los Angeles Dodgers	73–89	5th of 6	Fernando Valenzuela	Tom Lasorda
1987	Los Angeles Dodgers	73–89	4th of 6	Bob Welch	Tom Lasorda
1988	Los Angeles Dodgers	94–67	1st of 6	Orel Hershiser	Tom Lasorda
1989	Los Angeles Dodgers	77–83	4th of 6	Orel Hershiser	Tom Lasorda
1990	Los Angeles Dodgers	86–76	2nd of 6	Eddie Murray	Tom Lasorda
1991	Los Angeles Dodgers	93–69	2nd of 6	Brett Butler	Tom Lasorda
1992	Los Angeles Dodgers	63–99	6th of 6	Brett Butler	Tom Lasorda
1993	Los Angeles Dodgers	81–81	4th of 7	Mike Piazza	Tom Lasorda

Year	Team	Record	Place	Best Player	Manager
1994	Los Angeles Dodgers	58–56	1st of 4	Kevin Gross	Tom Lasorda
1995	Los Angeles Dodgers	78–66	1st of 4	Mike Piazza	Tom Lasorda
1996	Los Angeles Dodgers	90–72	2nd of 4	Mike Piazza	Tom Lasorda/ Bill Russell
1997	Los Angeles Dodgers	88–74	2nd of 4	Mike Piazza	Bill Russell
1998	Los Angeles Dodgers	83–79	3rd of 5	Gary Sheffield	Bill Russell/ Glenn Hoffman
1999	Los Angeles Dodgers	77–85	3rd of 5	Kevin Brown	Davey Johnson
2000	Los Angeles Dodgers	86–76	2nd of 5	Kevin Brown	Davey Johnson
2001	Los Angeles Dodgers	86–76	3rd of 5	Shawn Green	Jim Tracy
2002	Los Angeles Dodgers	92–70	3rd of 5	Shawn Green	Jim Tracy
2003	Los Angeles Dodgers	85–77	2nd of 5	Kevin Brown	Jim Tracy
2004	Los Angeles Dodgers	93–69	1st of 5	Adrian Beltre	Jim Tracy
2005	Los Angeles Dodgers	71–91	4th of 5	Jeff Kent	Jim Tracy
2006	Los Angeles Dodgers	88–74	2nd of 5	Derek Lowe	Grady Little
2007	Los Angeles Dodgers	82–80	4th of 5	Brad Penny	Grady Little
2008	Los Angeles Dodgers	84–78	1st of 5	Chad Billingsley	Joe Torre
2009	Los Angeles Dodgers	95–67	1st of 5	Matt Kemp	Joe Torre
2010	Los Angeles Dodgers	80–82	4th of 5	Clayton Kershaw	Joe Torre
2011	Los Angeles Dodgers	82–79	3rd of 5	Matt Kemp	Don Mattingly
2012	Los Angeles Dodgers	86–76	2nd of 5	Clayton Kershaw	Don Mattingly
2013	Los Angeles Dodgers	92–70	1st of 5	Clayton Kershaw	Don Mattingly
2014	Los Angeles Dodgers	94–68	1st of 5	Clayton Kershaw	Don Mattingly
2015	Los Angeles Dodgers	92–70	1st of 5	Zack Greinke	Don Mattingly
2016	Los Angeles Dodgers	91–71	1st of 5	Clayton Kershaw	Dave Roberts
2017	Los Angeles Dodgers	104–58	1st of 5	Justin Turner	Dave Roberts
2018	Los Angeles Dodgers	92–71	1st of 5	Justin Turner	Dave Roberts
2019	Los Angeles Dodgers	106–56	1st of 5	Cody Bellinger	Dave Roberts
2020	Los Angeles Dodgers	43–17	1st of 5	Mookie Betts	Dave Roberts
2021	Los Angeles Dodgers	106–56	2nd of 5	Walker Buehler	Dave Roberts
2022	Los Angeles Dodgers	111–51	1st of 5	Mookie Betts	Dave Roberts

* Note: 1981 was a split-season strike year. Best player based on Win Above Replacement player stat.

Overall record: 5,610–4,662 with six World Series titles, 12 NL Pennants, and 27 playoff appearances.

Winners of Multiple Best Player Awards
Don Drysdale, 5
Clayton Kershaw, 5
Mike Piazza, 5
Kevin Brown, 3
Ron Cey, 3
Pedro Guerrero, 3
Sandy Koufax, 3
Don Sutton, 3
Brett Butler, 2
Shawn Green, 2
Orel Hershiser, 2
Fernando Valenzuela, 2
Matt Kemp, 2
Justin Turner, 2
Mookie Betts, 2

World Series Titles
1959 (defeated White Sox, 4–2)
1963 (defeated Yankees, 4–0)
1965 (defeated Twins, 4–3)
1981 (defeated Yankees, 4–2)
1988 (defeated A's, 4–1)
2020 (defeated Rays, 4–2)

NL Champions
1959
1963
1965
1966 (lost to Baltimore in World Series, 4–0)

1974 (defeated Pittsburgh in NLCS, 3–1; lost to Oakland in World
Series, 4–1)

1977 (defeated Philadelphia in NLCS, 3–1; lost to Yankees in World
Series, 4–2)

1978 (defeated Philadelphia in NLCS, 3–1; lost to Yankees in World
Series, 4–2)

1981 (defeated Montreal in NLCS, 3–2)

1988 (defeated Mets in NLCS, 4–3)

2017 (lost to Astros in World Series, 4–3)

2018 (lost to Red Sox in World Series, 4–1)

2020

NL West Champions

1974

1977

1978

1981 (defeated Houston in NLDS, 3–2)

1983 (lost to Philadelphia in NLCS, 3–1)

1985 (lost to St. Louis in NLCS, 4–2)

1995 (lost to Cincinnati in NLDS, 3–0)

2004 (lost to St. Louis in NLDS, 3–1)

2008 (defeated Cubs in NLDS, 3–0; lost to Philadelphia in NLCS, 4–1)

2009 (defeated St. Louis in NLDS, 3–0; lost to Philadelphia in NLCS,
4–1)

2013 (defeated Atlanta in NLDS, 3–1; lost to St. Louis in NLCS, 4–2)

2014 (lost to St. Louis in NLDS, 3–1)

2015 (lost to Mets in NLDS, 3–2)

2016 (defeated Washington in NLDS, 3–2; lost to Cubs in NLCS,
4–2)

2017

2018
2019 (lost NLDS to Washington, 3–2)
2020
2022 (lost to San Diego in NLDS, 3–1)

Wild-Card Champion
1996 (lost to Atlanta in NLDS, 3–0)
2006 (lost to Mets in NLDS, 3–0)

Dodgers Retired Numbers
1–Pee Wee Reese
2–Tommy Lasorda
4–Duke Snider
14–Gil Hodges
19–Jim Gilliam
20–Don Sutton
24–Walt Alston
32–Sandy Koufax
39–Roy Campanella
42–Jackie Robinson
53–Don Drysdale

L.A. Dodgers Finishing in the Top 10 in MVP Award Voting
2022 (Freeman, 4th; Betts, 5th)
2021 (Max Muncy, 10th)
2020 (Mookie Betts, 2nd; Corey Seager, 9th)
2019 (Cody Bellinger, winner)
2017 (Justin Turner, 8th; Cody Bellinger, 9th)
2016 (Corey Seager, 3rd; Justin Turner, 9th)
2015 (Zack Greinke, 7th; Clayton Kershaw, 10th)
2014 (Clayton Kershaw, winner; Adrian Gonzalez, 7th)

2013 (Clayton Kershaw, 7th; Hanley Ramirez, 8th)

2012 (Matt Kemp, 2nd)

2009 (Andre Ethier, 6th, Matt Kemp, 10th)

2008 (Manny Ramirez, 4th)

2004 (Adrian Beltre, 2nd)

2003 (Eric Gagne, 6th)

2002 (Shawn Green, 5th)

2001 (Shawn Green, 6th)

2000 (Gary Sheffield, 9th)

1997 (Mike Piazza, 2nd)

1996 (Mike Piazza, 2nd)

1995 (Mike Piazza, 4th; Eric Karros, 5th)

1994 (Mike Piazza, 6th)

1993 (Mike Piazza, 9th)

1991 (Brett Butler, 7th; Darryl Strawberry, 9th)

1990 (Eddie Murray, 5th)

1988 (Kirk Gibson, winner; Orel Hershiser, 6th)

1985 (Pedro Guerrero, 3rd)

1983 (Pedro Guerrero, 4th)

1982 (Pedro Guerrero, 3rd)

1981 (Fernando Valenzuela, 5th; Dusty Baker, 7th)

1980 (Dusty Baker, 4th; Steve Garvey, 6th)

1978 (Steve Garvey, 2nd; Reggie Smith, 4th)

1977 (Reggie Smith, 4th; Steve Garvey, 6th; Ron Cey, 8th)

1976 (Steve Garvey, 6th)

1974 (Steve Garvey, winner; Mike Marshall, 3rd; Jim Wynn, 5th)

1971 (Maury Wills, 6th; Al Downing, 10th)

1970 (Wes Parker, 5th)

1966 (Sandy Koufax, 2nd; Phil Regan, 7th)

1965 (Sandy Koufax, 2nd; Maury Wills, 3rd; Don Drysdale, 5th)

1963 (Sandy Koufax, winner; Ron Perranoski, 4th; Jim Gilliam, 6th; Tommy Davis, 8th)
1962 (Maury Wills, winner; Tommy Davis, 3rd; Don Drysdale, 5th; Frank Howard, 9th)
1961 (Maury Wills, 9th)
1959 (Wally Moon, 4th; Charlie Neal, 8th)

L.A. Dodgers Finishing in the Top 10 in Cy Young Award Voting

2022 (Julio Urias, 3rd)
2021 (Walker Buehler, 4th; Julio Urias, 7th)
2020 (Clayton Kershaw, 9th)
2019 (Hyun-jin Ryu, 2nd; Clayton Kershaw, 8th; Walker Buehler, 9th)
2017 (Clayton Kershaw, 2nd; Kenley Jansen, 5th; Alex Wood, 9th)
2016 (Clayton Kershaw, 5th)
2015 (Zack Greinke, 2nd; Clayton Kershaw, 3rd)
2014 (Clayton Kershaw, winner; Zack Greinke, 7th)
2013 (Clayton Kershaw, 1st; Zack Greinke, 8th)
2012 (Clayton Kershaw, 2nd)
2011 (Clayton Kershaw, winner)
2007 (Brad Penny, 3rd)
2006 (Takashi Saito, 8th)
2004 (Eric Gagne, 7th)
2003 (Eric Gagne, winner)
2002 (Eric Gagne, 4th)
2000 (Kevin Brown, 6th)
1999 (Kevin Brown, 6th)
1996 (Hideo Nomo, 4th; Todd Worrell, tied for 5th)
1995 (Hideo Nomo, 4th; Ramon Martinez, 5th)
1990 (Ramon Martinez, 2nd)
1989 (Orel Hershiser, tied for 4th; Tim Belcher, tied for 6th)
1988 (Orel Hershiser, winner)

1987 (Orel Hershiser, 4th)

1986 (Fernando Valenzuela, 2nd)

1985 (Orel Hershiser, 3rd; Fernando Valenzuela, 6th)

1983 (Bob Welch, 8th)

1982 (Fernando Valenzuela, tied for 3rd)

1981 (Fernando Valenzuela, winner)

1980 (Jerry Reuss, 2nd)

1978 (Burt Hooton, 2nd; Tommy John, tied for 8th)

1977 (Tommy John, 2nd)

1976 (Don Sutton, 3rd)

1975 (Don Sutton and Andy Messersmith, tied for 5th)

1974 (Mike Marshall, winner; Andy Messersmith, 2nd; Don Sutton, 4th)

1973 (Don Sutton, 5th)

1972 (Don Sutton, tied for 5th)

1971 (Al Downing, 3rd)

1966 (Sandy Koufax, winner)

1965 (Sandy Koufax, winner)

1964 (Sandy Koufax, 3rd)

1963 (Sandy Koufax, winner)

1962 (Don Drysdale, winner)

L.A. Dodgers Finishing in the Top 10 in Rookie of the Year Voting

2020 (Tony Gonsolin, 4th; Dustin May, 5th)

2018 (Walker Buehler, 3rd)

2017 (Cody Bellinger, winner)

2016 (Corey Seager, winner; Kenta Maeda, 3rd)

2015 (Joc Pederson, tied for 6th)

2013 (Yasiel Puig, 2nd; Hyun-jin Ryu, 4th)

2011 (Kenley Jansen, tied for 7th)

2007 (James Loney, tied for 6th)

2006 (Takashi Saito, tied for 7th; Russell Martin, tied for 9th)

2002 (Kaz Ishii, 4th)

1996 (Todd Hollandsworth, winner)

1995 (Hideo Nomo, winner; Ismael Valdez, tied for 7th)

1994 (Raul Mondesi, winner)

1993 (Mike Piazza, winner; Pedro Martinez, tied for 9th)

1992 (Eric Karros, winner)

1988 (Tim Belcher, 3rd)

1985 (Mariano Duncan, 3rd)

1984 (Orel Hershiser, 3rd)

1983 (Greg Brock, tied for 7th)

1982 (Steve Sax, winner)

1981 (Fernando Valenzuela, winner)

1980 (Steve Howe, winner)

1979 (Rick Sutcliffe, winner)

1973 (Ron Cey and Davey Lopes, tied for 6th)

1969 (Ted Sizemore, winner)

1965 (Jim Lefebvre, winner)

1960 (Frank Howard, winner; Tommy Davis, 5th)

L.A. Dodgers Finishing in the Top 10 in Manager of the Year Voting

2022 (Dave Roberts, 2nd)

2021 (Dave Roberts, 5th)

2020 (Dave Roberts, 5th)

2019 (Dave Roberts, 4th)

2018 (Dave Roberts, 6th)

2017 (Dave Roberts, 2nd)

2016 (Dave Roberts, winner)

2015 (Don Mattingly, tied for 5th)

2014 (Don Mattingly, 6th)

2013 (Don Mattingly, 2nd)

2011 (Don Mattingly, tied for 8th)

2009 (Joe Torre, 3rd)

2008 (Joe Torre, 4th)

2006 (Grady Little, 4th)

2004 (Jim Tracy, 3rd)

2002 (Jim Tracy, 4th)

2001 (Jim Tracy, 2nd)

1996 (Bill Russell, 5th)

1994 (Tommy Lasorda, tied for 5th)

1991 (Tommy Lasorda, 4th)

1990 (Tommy Lasorda, 3rd)

1988 (Tommy Lasorda, winner)

1985 (Tommy Lasorda, 3rd)

1983 (Tommy Lasorda, winner)

Note: Manager of the Year was first handed out in 1983

Gold Glove Awards

1958 Gil Hodges, 1b

1959 Gil Hodges, 1b; Charlie Neal, 2b

1960 Wally Moon, of

1961 John Roseboro, c; Maury Wills, ss

1962 Maury Wills, ss

1967 Wes Parker, 1b

1968 Wes Parker, 1b

1969 Wes Parker, 1b

1970 Wes Parker, 1b

1971 Wes Parker, 1b; Willie Davis, of

1972 Wes Parker, 1b; Willie Davis, of

1973 Willie Davis, of

1974 Andy Messersmith, p; Steve Garvey, 1b

1975 Andy Messersmith, p; Steve Garvey, 1b

1976 Steve Garvey, 1b
1977 Steve Garvey, 1b
1978 Davey Lopes, 2b
1981 Dusty Baker, of
1986 Fernando Valenzuela, p
1988 Orel Hershiser, p
1995 Raul Mondesi, of
1997 Raul Mondesi, of
1998 Charles Johnson, c
2004 Cesar Izturis, ss; Steve Finley, of
2006 Greg Maddux, p
2007 Russell Martin, c
2009 Orlando Hudson, 2b; Matt Kemp, of
2011 Clayton Kershaw, p; Matt Kemp, of; Andre Ethier, of
2014 Adrian Gonzalez, 1b; Zack Greinke, p
2015 Zack Greinke, p
2019 Cody Bellinger, rf
2020 Mookie Betts, rf
2022 Mookie Betts, rf

NLCS MVP
1977 Dusty Baker
1978 Steve Garvey
1981 Burt Hooton
1988 Orel Hershiser
2017 Justin Turner and Chris Taylor
2018 Cody Bellinger
2020 Corey Seager

World Series MVP
1959 Larry Sherry
1963 Sandy Koufax
1965 Sandy Koufax
1981 Ron Cey, Pedro Guerrero and Steve Yeager
1988 Orel Hershiser
2020 Corey Seager

All-Star Game MVP
1962 Maury Wills (first game)
1974 Steve Garvey
1977 Don Sutton
1978 Steve Garvey
1996 Mike Piazza

NL Comeback Player of the Year
2006 Nomar Garciaparra

NL Batting Champions
1962 Tommy Davis (.346)
1963 Tommy Davis (.326)
2021 Trea Turner (.328)

NL Lowest ERA
1962 Sandy Koufax (2.54)
1963 Sandy Koufax (1.88)
1964 Sandy Koufax (1.74)
1965 Sandy Koufax (2.04)
1966 Sandy Koufax (1.73)
1980 Don Sutton (2.20)
1984 Alejandro Pena (2.48)

2000 Kevin Brown (2.58)
2011 Clayton Kershaw (2.28)
2012 Clayton Kershaw (2.53)
2013 Clayton Kershaw (1.83)
2014 Clayton Kershaw (1.77)
2015 Zack Greinke (1.66)
2017 Clayton Kershaw (2.31)
2019 Hyun-jin Ryu (2.32)
2021 Julio Urias (2.29)
2022 Julio Urias (2.16)

L.A. Dodger All-Time Leaders
Homers
1. Eric Karros, 270
2. Ron Cey, 228
3. Steve Garvey, 211
4. Matt Kemp, 203
5. Mike Piazza, 177
6. Pedro Guerrero, 171
7. Raul Mondesi, 163
8. Andre Ethier, 162
8. Shawn Green, 162
10. Justin Turner, 156

Hits
1. Willie Davis, 2,091
2. Steve Garvey, 1,968
3. Bill Russell 1,926
4. Maury Wills, 1,732
5. Eric Karros, 1,608
6. Ron Cey, 1,378

7. Andre Ethier, 1,367
8. Matt Kemp, 1,322
9. Steve Sax, 1,218
10. Davey Lopes, 1,204

Stolen Bases
1. Maury Wills, 490
2. Davey Lopes, 418
3. Willie Davis, 335
4. Steve Sax, 290
5. Brett Butler, 179
6. Matt Kemp, 170
7. Bill Russell, 167
8. Raul Mondesi, 140
9. Juan Pierre, 134
10. Dee Gordon, 130

Wins Above Replacement
1. Clayton Kershaw, 73.1
2. Willie Davis, 54.6
3. Don Drysdale, 53.6
4. Sandy Koufax, 51.2
5. Don Sutton, 50.5
6. Ron Cey, 47.7
7. Orel Hershiser, 39.6
8. Steve Garvey, 36.6
9. Justin Turner, 34.0
10. Fernando Valenzuela, 33.0

Wins

1. Don Sutton, 233
2. Clayton Kershaw, 197
3. Don Drysdale, 187
4. Sandy Koufax, 156
5. Claude Osteen, 147
6. Fernando Valenzuela, 141
7. Orel Hershiser, 135
8. Ramon Martinez, 123
9. Bob Welch, 115
10. Burt Hooton, 112

ERA

1. Clayton Kershaw, 2.48
2. Sandy Koufax, 2.64
3. Tommy John, 2.97
4. Don Drysdale, 2.98
5. Bill Singer, 3.03
6. Claude Osteen, 3.09
7. Don Sutton, 3.09
8. Jerry Reuss, 3.11
9. Orel Hershiser, 3.12
10. Burt Hooton, 3.14

Strikeouts

1. Clayton Kershaw, 2,807
2. Don Sutton, 2,696
3. Don Drysdale, 2,283
4. Sandy Koufax, 2,214
5. Fernando Valenzuela, 1,759
6. Orel Hershiser, 1,456

7. Ramon Martinez, 1,314
8. Bob Welch, 1,292
9. Hideo Nomo, 1,200
10. Chan Ho Park, 1,177

Saves

1. Kenley Jansen, 350
2. Eric Gagne, 161
3. Jeff Shaw, 129
4. Todd Worrell, 127
5. Jim Brewer, 126
6. Ron Perranoski, 100
7. Jay Howell, 85
8. Jonathan Broxton, 84
9. Takashi Saito, 81
10. Tom Niedenfuer, 64

SOURCES

Books

Bouton, Jim. *Ball Four: The 20th Anniversary Edition*. Hoboken, NJ: Wiley, 1990.

Delsohn, Steve. *True Blue*. New York: Harper Perennial, 2002.

Gibson, Kirk and Lynn Henning. *Bottom of the Ninth*. Ann Arbor, MI: Sleeping Bear Press, 1997.

Haddad, Paul. *High Fives, Pennant Drives and Fernandomania*. Solana Beach, CA: Santa Monica Press, 2012.

Hershiser, Orel and Jerry B. Jenkins. *Out of the Blue*. Orlando, FL: Wolgemuth and Hyatt, 1989.

Lasorda, Tom and David Fisher. *The Artful Dodger*. New York: Avon Books, 1986.

Lyle, Sparky and Peter Golenbock. *The Bronx Zoo*. New York: Dell, 1980.

Plaschke, Bill and Tommy Lasorda. *I Live for This!* New York: Mariner Books, 2010.

Strawberry, Darryl. *Straw: Finding My Way*. Sulphur Springs, TX: Ecco, 2009.

Suchon, Josh. *Miracle Men: Hershiser, Gibson and the Improbable 1988 Dodgers*. Chicago: Triumph Books, 2013.

Weisman, Jon. *100 Things Dodgers Fans Should Know & Do Before They Die*. Chicago: Triumph Books, 2009.

Websites

www.latimes.com/sports

www.sfgate.com

www.nytimes.com

www.baseball-reference.com

www.baseball-almanac.com

www.sinatra.com

www.espn.com

www.mlb.com

www.dodgers.com

ABOUT THE AUTHOR

Houston Mitchell has worked for the *Los Angeles Times* sports department since 1991 and was promoted to assistant sports editor in 2009. He has written the popular Dodgers Dugout newsletter for them since 2015. You can sign up at latimes.com/newsletters/dodgers-dugout. He has been a Dodgers fan for as long as he can remember and lives happily in San Dimas, California, with his wife, three kids, and four dogs.